THE WORLD'S FIGHTERS

THE WORLD'S
FIGHTERS

H. F. KING

 FOLLETT PUBLISHING COMPANY/CHICAGO

First published 1971 in Great Britain by
The Bodley Head Ltd.
Follett edition published 1973

ISBN 695-80376-X

Library of Congress Catalog Card Number: 72-94774

CONTENTS

ACKNOWLEDGMENTS

Three of the photographs appearing in this book were kindly supplied by *Flight International* (pages 43 and 119), and the Ministry of Defence (page 115).

INTRODUCTION: WHY FIGHT?

Fighting in the air began in 1914, but the idea of it goes back through the centuries, even, it seems, to mythology. Can it be denied that aerobatics, the spectacular acrobatic-like manoeuvres which came to be used by the pilots of fighting aeroplanes to aim their guns, or evade pursuit by other fighters, were vividly suggested in this description by Nathaniel Hawthorne of the struggle between Pegasus the flying horse and his would-be master Bellerophon? 'He reared himself erect, with his forelegs on a wreath of mist, and his hind legs on nothing at all. He flung out his heels behind, and put down his head between his legs, with his wings pointing upward. At about two miles' height above the earth he turned a somersault, so that Bellerophon's heels were where his head should have been, and he seemed to look down into the sky, instead of up.'

Even in the First World War fighters were somersaulting, or looping, at heights well above two miles.

The idea of air fighting remained in men's minds, and in the early 1500s the Dutch artist Jerome Bosch depicted, in *The Temptation of St Anthony*, fabulous aerial craft 'grappling in the central blue'. This was a phrase used by Alfred, Lord Tennyson when he wrote in 1842 of 'the nations' airy navies', or the great air forces of the future.

In the later years of Queen Victoria's reign imaginative writers, of whom H. G. Wells was one, described formidable aircraft, armed with guns and joining battle in terrible wars; and prominent among these writers was George Griffith, father of Dr A. A. Griffith. Together with Sir Frank Whittle, Dr Griffith pioneered the gas turbine and compressor for aircraft. These are the principal parts of the turbojet engine, later described as the powerplant used in today's jet-propelled fighters.

Although air battles had been imagined, when war came in 1914 the opposing Powers little thought that they would actually occur, and were certainly poorly equipped for them. One reason for this is that the chief duty of the aeroplane was considered to be that of reconnaissance, or the gathering of information about happenings on the ground; and this is understandable, because balloons had been used for this same purpose since the Battle of Fleurus in Belgium in 1794.

Even before 1914 it had been realised that enemy reconnaissance aircraft would have to be intercepted, or met in the air, and prevented from completing their task. Bombing raids would also have to be met, for Italian aeroplanes had dropped bombs in war during 1911–12. The first duty of the fighting aeroplane, or fighter, was, then, to deny to the enemy the freedom to undertake reconnaissance and bombing flights by destroying the intruding aircraft. Next the fighter had to deal with other fighters which sought to protect the intruders.

As the war progressed, massive fighter-versus-fighter battles developed – frantic dogfights wherein heroism, skill and even chivalry found a new place in warfare, as well as the technical quality of aircraft, engines and weapons. These battles decided which side should hold air superiority, air supremacy or command of the air, and generally took place over the areas of the great land battles. As the First World War drew to its end, however, British fighters were being fitted with extra petrol tanks, the intention being that they should penetrate with bombers deep into enemy territory in raids on centres of war production. These long-range escort or penetration fighters were special versions of the Sopwith Snipe and Martinsyde Buzzard. They were never actually used; but they were the true ancestors of the far-ranging Mustangs, Lightnings and Thunderbolts which struck into the heart of Germany with the American bomber formations after 1943.

Over the span of their development fighters were adapted to attack ground targets, using bombs as well as their guns. They were adapted also for reconnaissance on behalf of the ground forces (fighter reconnaissance or tactical reconnaissance), and, stripped of armament, were equipped for long-range photographic reconnaissance (PR). Special equipment enabled them to operate from naval craft of various kinds. They were fitted with floats and skis and some were launched from, and taken aboard, other aircraft. These developments will be touched upon in later pages; but the first aim is to show how the fighter aircraft itself was developed into the deadly hunter/killer it is today.

Three generations of British fighters, all built by the Gloster ▶
company. Nearest the camera is a Gladiator, the prototype of which
was first flown in 1934. The centre aircraft is a Meteor night
fighter, developed from the original Meteor of 1943, and uppermost
is a Javelin, a type built to a specification issued in 1948 but which
did not enter service until 1956.

1

Early Ideas

Historians are very uncertain when a gun was first mounted on an aeroplane, but the present writer firmly believes that the date was towards the end of 1910 and that the aircraft concerned was a French Voisin biplane of pusher type. A pusher aircraft is one having the airscrew, or propeller, mounted at the rear, the tail being usually carried on booms, or pole-like members, attached to the wings. This somewhat ungainly structure made the type comparatively slow.

The gun on the 1910 Voisin was a very big one indeed, and might have been more at home on a torpedo-boat destroyer or light cruiser. Fortunately there is no reason to suppose that this particular installation was ever tested in the air, and this is certainly to be hoped, for the sake of the pilot and gunner. The recoil, or rearward kick, of such a gun would have been very heavy, and might have had a sad effect on the structure of the aircraft. Nevertheless, a gun of 37-mm calibre – that is, one having a barrel measuring about 37 mm in its internal diameter, or bore – was certainly fired from a Voisin pusher biplane before war came in 1914. This is remarkable, for the gun (or cannon, as guns of 15-mm calibre or over will now be called) fired a shell about five times as big as an ordinary machine-gun bullet of rifle calibre. By this last expression is meant a bullet as used in an ordinary military rifle and commonly of about 0·303 in or 7–8-mm bore or calibre.

Somewhat earlier, in August 1910, a firearm was first discharged from an aeroplane in flight. The weapon was a US Army Springfield rifle, and it was fired from a Curtiss pusher biplane. The earliest firing of a machine-gun in the air was almost certainly

◀ Nose and cockpit of the Sopwith Snipe, with the muzzles of the two Vickers machine-guns showing above the engine cowling. As noted in the Introduction, fighters of this type were adapted for long-range escort work.

done from a Wright pusher biplane in June 1912. The gun was of the Lewis type, a light, handy weapon then recently invented. This same type of gun was to be very widely used on aircraft in later years.

Just over a year later a mechanism enabling a gun fixed to an aircraft to fire between the blades of a revolving tractor airscrew (one located at the front) without damaging the blades was patented by a German named Franz Schneider; but a device of this sort was not developed to a usable state until 1915. After that time such devices became known as synchronising or interrupter gears. With such a gear the entire aircraft had to be aimed directly at the target, or, if there were large relative movements between the two aircraft concerned, at the point in space where the stream of bullets would meet the target. When allowance was made for such movements the fighter pilot was said to allow for deflection.

Until gun gears of the type mentioned had been perfected the pusher type of aeroplane was attractive as a platform for a free gun, that is, a gun capable of being elevated or depressed (aimed up or down) or traversed (swung round). In this type of aircraft the gunner could be stationed in the nose of the nacelle, or the short body serving the purpose of the fuselage of a tractor aircraft, and housing the pilot, gunner and engine. Here he could command a wide field of fire, an expression meaning the area over which he could fire his gun without fear of damaging his own aircraft.

In the British Military Aeroplane Trials, which took place on Salisbury Plain in 1912, no demands whatever were made for the mounting of a gun, and the authorities noted that only in one of the thirty-two entries – a machine known as the Mersey Monoplane – had an 'endeavour been made to fit the design to the requirements of actual war.' For this aircraft, which met a tragic end during the contest, the designer claimed in 1911: 'First, the occupants have an uninterrupted view in front; secondly, the engine being immediately in front, it nicely warms the car, a very great advantage in cold weather; thirdly, the engine being in front, in case of an accident, the men fall on the engine instead of the engine on the men. Lastly, the propeller being in the stern, there is very much less draught on the occupants, and the entire front is open to the gaze or to throwing things out without any fear of injuring the propeller.'

'Throwing things out' could well have included bullets; but no gun was ever installed on the Mersey Monoplane, and perhaps the first aeroplane specially designed for attacking other aeroplanes was another British type, the Vickers E.F.B.1 *Destroyer*, first exhibited at the Olympia Aero Show held in London in 1913. This pusher biplane not only carried a machine-gun in the nose of the nacelle but was clearly designed to achieve a high performance, a term which embraces speed; rate of climb; ceiling, or maximum height attainable; and other quantities.

Months before the coming of war in 1914 Britain, as well as France, was experimenting with aircraft cannon firing shells weighing $1-1\frac{1}{2}$ lb, though guns of this large size were never to become common on fighters. It may be noted at this point that in the tables which accompany the later chapters, the following contractions are used under the heading 'Armament': 'r-c m-g' = rifle-calibre machine-gun; 'h m-g' = heavy machine-gun, meaning a gun of about $\frac{1}{2}$-in calibre; 'c' = cannon, or guns of a size already defined and generally capable of firing explosive shells; 'u-g m' = unguided missile; 'g m' = guided missile. The nature of these last-named weapons will later be described.

A warning is necessary concerning performance figures. It is often tempting to take sheer speed as a measure of a fighter's efficiency; but speed must be set against such considerations as rate of climb; manoeuvrability, or the ability to change direction swiftly; speed and steadiness in a dive; acceleration (just as in a car); fighting view; ease of maintenance under active-service conditions; and ease of refuelling and rearming, a term which means taking a fresh ammunition supply aboard, be it in the form of bullets for machine-guns, explosive shells for cannon, unguided missiles or guided missiles. These are just a few of the considerations in designing a fighter. The figures given in the tables must, in any case, be approximate, for fighters appear with many variations of engine and equipment. In the early years especially, performance could be affected to a marked extent by the age of the aircraft (the fabric covering, for example, losing its taughtness); how it was rigged, or trued-up for flight by the riggers; and – all too frequently – how well the engine had been attended to by the mechanics. Finally, the term service ceiling is defined as the height at which engine power, or, in the case of a turbojet engine, thrust, has decreased to such an extent, owing to the rarified air, that the rate of climb has fallen off to only a hundred feet a minute.

Other methods than gunnery were proposed before the 1914–18 war for attacking aircraft, especially airships. These included the trailing of grapnels, or anchor-like devices; the firing or throwing of grenades, or small bombs as used by the Army and Navy; and the discharging (at the suggestion of a First Lord of the Admiralty in 1913) of 'a series of bombs or fireballs, at rapid intervals, so that a string of them, more than a hundred yards in length, would be drawn like a whiplash across the gasbag.' What occurred in reality is now described.

2

First World War: August 1914–April 1917

The bold experiments in air gunnery referred to in the preceding chapter were, after all, only experiments, and when Germany invaded Belgium on 4 August 1914, the prospects of, and preparations for, widespread air fighting were almost non-existent. Aware of this fact, the French designer/constructor Gabriel Voisin, whose name has already been mentioned in connection with a gun installation of 1910, made what amounted to a personal raid on the Hotchkiss machine-gun factory to procure some guns for mounting on Voisin pusher biplanes for the French Air Force. Voisin's foresight and determination did not go unrewarded: with the war only a few weeks old, on 5 October 1914, a Voisin biplane piloted by Sgt Franz, and with a mechanic named Quénault as gunner, shot down a German aeroplane. Although the weapon used was a Hotchkiss machine-

gun it did not function as such on this occasion. Doubting the reliability of the automatic mechanism, Quénault fired single shots only, forty-seven in fact – before the gun jammed at the forty-eighth. Then, as he tried to clear the jam, the mechanic saw his target crash to earth.

Yet even this early combat was not the first occasion on which an aeroplane was forced down by gunfire from another, though it was doubtless the first in which a machine-gun was successfully employed. Lieut-Col C. W. Wilson has described how, as a 2nd-Lieut in Britain's Royal Flying Corps, he was ordered to take-off in pursuit of an approaching Taube – an early type of German monoplane used for reconnaissance. The British aircraft was an Avro 504 biplane, and before Wilson could get into the rear cockpit a Lieut Rabagliatti had clambered into the front cockpit with a rifle and ammunition. 'We headed north, climbing,' Wilson has recorded, 'Rabagliatti kneeling on his seat in front and steering me until we got into position ahead and below as we had always meant to do. He then began firing and ejecting his empties into my face, cursing at the lack of result. Suddenly his face lit up, and waving his rifle in the air he pointed to the ground . . . We were credited with the *first* German machine in the official history of the Royal Flying Corps.' The date of that historic victory was 25 August 1914.

The problem of disposing of the empties – the spent cartridge-cases – was one that was to remain for many years after machine-guns had been generally fitted to fighters. But there were far bigger problems concerning armament. As none of the aeroplanes used in the earliest phase of the war had been designed for fighting or to carry a machine-gun, and as, in any case, suitable light machine-guns were at that time scarce, many kinds of weapons had to be pressed into service. Automatic pistols and revolvers were popular because they were easily handled in the air. Rifles, especially of the short carbine type designed for cavalry use, were also employed, sometimes having the wooden stock removed for lightness and being fixed to the aircraft. Shotguns of sporting type were also taken aloft, and even loaded with chain-shot of the type used in

Nelson's time to destroy the rigging of enemy ships. With their multitude of wires, which served to brace, or stiffen, the wing structure, the aeroplanes of 1914 had much in common with the ships at Trafalgar. The Germans were fortunate in having a supply of automatic rifles of the Mexican Mondragon type, originally intended for the army but very suitable for air fighting because of their high rate of fire. Grenades too, found a place in the aerial armoury, and there was at least one instance of a pilot, Lieut N. C. Spratt, RFC, tying a grenade to a length of control cable with the intention of towing the grenade into the airscrew of an opponent. This device was never used, but on one occasion, when Spratt had taken aboard a supply of steel darts as the armament of his Sopwith Tabloid, he forced an enemy aircraft to land – not by showering it with darts, but by manoeuvring in an aggressive manner. Often the grenades were of the type designed to be fired from a rifle, and these were among the earliest weapons carried by British pilots for attacking airships. One of these pilots recalls going out in a Maurice Farman biplane 'to hunt Zeppelins, armed with a rifle and rifle grenades', explaining: 'I think a certain amount of confusion existed in my mind as to whether to throw them or shoot them. Word had gone forth that a certain gallant commanding officer had ruled that in the event of neither the shooting nor the throwing attaining the desired result, the alternative form of attack should consist of ramming the airship head on. What with one thing and another I was glad not to encounter any.'

The arming of fighters for attacks on airships became an acute problem and will be touched upon again, especially in connection with the raids on the British Isles; but the development of the true fighting aeroplane was to be observed during 1915 over the Western Front. That this class of aircraft was known to the British throughout the war as scout may be best explained by further reference to the Sopwith Tabloid. This was a tiny single-seat biplane, first built before the war for sporting and scouting purposes. Insofar as its military use was concerned it was what might be known today as a high-speed reconnaissance aircraft. Similar British types were the Bristol Scout and Martinsyde S.1, and the true forerunner of the class was the B.S.1 built at the Royal Aircraft Factory, Farnborough, as early as 1912. A comparable German type was the Fokker single-seat monoplane, and France had the Morane-Saulnier monoplane in the same category.

By virtue of their speed and rate of climb such aircraft as these were obvious choices for chasing or hunting other aeroplanes, and this explains the French term avion de chasse and the German Jagdflugzeuge. In later years the Americans, many of whose pilots fought and trained with the French, adopted the term pursuit, as represented by the 'P' designations of American fighters which will be described later.

Although the British, French and German single-seaters previously mentioned had a performance which made them suitable for fighting they were all of tractor type. As no synchronising gear was at first available British fighters were often armed with a Lewis gun, the bulky cooling jacket of which had been removed for lightness, fixed to the side of the fuselage, pointing outward to clear the revolving airscrew blades; but this meant that the pilot had to engage his target crab-fashion. Sometimes the gun was fixed to the top wing and fired above the airscrew, but the changing of ammunition magazines then became difficult. Quite clearly, the full development of the fighter had to await the coming of synchronising gear.

A German patent for a mechanism of this kind has already been mentioned and there was early interest also in France, where an aircraft engineer named Raymond Saulnier made experiments which failed. One of the reasons for this failure was that some of the cartridges hung fire, or failed to explode as quickly as they should, so that some of the bullets hit the airscrew. This led Saulnier to fix a steel plate on each blade to turn these bullets aside. Develop-

Though seen in captivity this Fokker E.III still bears its original markings. The form of cross shown was later changed by the Germans to a straight-sided variety.

ment of the main system had to be abandoned, but the deflector plates were retained, and with a Morane-Saulnier Type N monoplane so equipped the famous French pilot Roland Garros went into action in the spring of 1915. After a number of successes in combat Garros was forced to land behind the German lines, and the airscrew thus captured came to the attention of the Dutch designer Anthony Fokker, who was working for the Germans. Fokker did not copy the system of deflector plates, but it stimulated his own ideas, and, together with two of his technicians, he produced a workable synchronising gear, utilising a linkage of cams and push-rods between the oil-pump drive on the engine and the firing mechanism of the gun. This Stangensteuerung (push-rod control) gear was applied to the Fokker monoplane, which entered service as the E.I.

The pilot most closely associated with the E.I, or

with the more powerful sub-types developed from it (the E.IV had two guns) was Max Immelmann. Others were Oswald Boelcke and Ernst Udet, a leader of the German Air Force in the Second World War. Instant successes were achieved, and new tactics, or methods of attack and defence, were evolved. The most famous of these was the Immelmann turn, which enabled a Fokker pilot to gain height and reverse direction very quickly.

Now came the 'Fokker scourge', one of the most significant occurrences in the history of air warfare, and one which led, on 14 January 1916, to the issuing of an order from RFC headquarters declaring: 'Until the Royal Flying Corps are in possession of a machine as good as or better than the German Fokker it seems that a change in the tactics employed becomes necessary. It is hoped very shortly to obtain a machine which will be able to successfully engage the Fokkers . . . In the meantime it must be laid down that a machine proceeding on reconnaissance must be escorted by at least three other fighting machines.'

With the E.I the true fighter was now on the scene, and a deadly menace it was.

For ultimate victory over the 'Fokker scourge' three types of Allied fighters were mainly responsible: the French Nieuport Baby tractor, with a machine-gun on the top wing, firing over the airscrew, and the British D.H.2 and F.E.2b, both of which were of

pusher type. The D.H.2 was a single-seater with a Lewis gun in the nose. As at first installed this gun had a certain freedom of movement for aiming, but as experience was gained the British pilots preferred to have the gun fixed to fire along the line of flight. The F.E.2b was a two-seater, with a gunner in the nose, a position giving him a very wide field of fire for his free Lewis gun or guns, for sometimes two were fitted. In the latter case the second gun was on a telescopic pillar mounting, enabling the gunner, by a considerable feat of gymnastics, to stand and fire to the rear above the pilot's head. Despite its large size (the wing span was nearly 50 ft, whereas that of the D.H.2 was less than 30 ft) the F.E.2b proved a true fighter, especially during the Battle of the Somme, in the summer of 1916. Numbered among its victims was the great Max Immelmann. The F.E.2d was more powerful and faster.

It may well be wondered at this point what had become of the descendants of the Vickers *Destroyer*, which had a place of honour in the preceding chapter. Two developments of the type, the F.B.5 and F.B.9, both generally known as 'Gun Bus', were indeed taken into service, and one F.B.5 was in action against a German aircraft which flew up the River Thames as early as Christmas Day 1914. The F.B.5 gained respect among German pilots. Clearly, however, the pusher type of aeroplane could never

An Italian-built Nieuport XI Baby. Italian markings – red, white and green stripes – are painted on the tail
and a Lewis gun is carried over the top wing.

match the speeds now coming into prospect for the tractor type, although the tractor was never to compare with the pusher in the field of vision it afforded. More than one otherwise excellent fighter of later years was rendered largely useless by restricted outlook for the pilot.

One other factor which had a definite influence on the development of fighters was the type and power of the engine selected. The compact air-cooled rotary type, which revolved like a Catherine wheel, was at first favoured by all the rival designers, but with the introduction during the winter of 1916 of their Albatros D.I the Germans began to show a marked preference for the water-cooled inline type,

A truly valiant war-horse was the F.E.2d, lumbering in appearance but formidable in combat. This example has three Lewis guns, and the gunner is demonstrating the use of a camera.

with cylinders arranged one behind the other instead of radiating outwards from the centre like the petals of a sunflower, as in the rotary type. The Albatros

D.I was a replacement for the history-making Fokker monoplanes and for the Halberstadt biplanes which had joined them in service. It was, in fact, the Halberstadts which had marked the beginning of the German trend towards the water-cooled engine. Although relatively heavy and long the inline type of engine offered opportunities for a very clean, or streamlined, installation, though the disposition of the radiator presented something of a problem. On the Albatros D.I the radiator for the Benz or Mercedes engine was divided into two sections, one on each side, an arrangement which permitted the nose of the aircraft to be made of very good streamline form, with a quite massive spinner, or streamlined cap, over the airscrew hub. The D.I was also remarkable for its fuselage construction, for, although the framework was of wood, as on preceding fighters (with the notable exception of the Fokker monoplane, which had a steel-tube framework), the covering was also of wood, instead of the usual fabric. With their relatively powerful engines the Albatros D.I, and the somewhat refined D.II, had an excellent rate of climb, and among their pilots was the most famous German airman of all, Baron Manfred von Richthofen.

France, too, was beginning to show a preference for the water-cooled engine, and this was apparent when the SPAD VII began to enter service in the

An early example of the Vickers Gun Bus. The 'pusher' arrangement permitted a wide field of fire for a gun, which was mounted on the pedestal seen in the extreme nose.

winter of 1916. This was one of the outstanding fighters of the war, as indicated by the fact that it was flown not only by French, but by British, Italian, Belgian and American pilots also. One British pilot has said: 'It was an eminently French machine – sensitive, neat, elegant to look at, demanding skill from its pilots and amply repaying the exercise of skill.' The SPAD VII, which gradually replaced the

Seen on top of the fuselage of this Sopwith 1½ Strutter, ahead of the front cockpit, is the pilot's Vickers gun. The man in the Scarff ring-mounting is aiming the Lewis gun.

Nieuport Baby in squadron service, was armed with a Vickers gun, lying ahead of the cockpit and firing above the nose-mounted radiator for the Hispano-Suiza vee-type engine. This type of engine had its two rows of cylinders arranged in the form of the letter V.

Among British fighters the air-cooled rotary engine continued to be favoured, and this was the powerplant of two Sopwith types, both of which achieved distinction. The first of these was the 1½ Strutter, so called because of the unusual arrangement of the wing-bracing struts. This fighter was a two-seater, but very different in layout from its predecessors the Gun Bus and F.E.2b. It was, in fact, of tractor type, and as by the time of its introduction into service in the spring of 1916 British gun-synchronising mechanisms were becoming available, the pilot, as well as the gunner, had a gun. This was of the Vickers type, similar in principle to that installed on the Vickers *Destroyer* of 1913. Being belt-fed, that is, having the cartridges delivered to it in a continuous belt, the gun did not require the pilot to change ammunition magazines, or cartridge containers, as on the drum-fed Lewis gun. The cartridges for the Lewis gun were contained in a circular drum, or pan, fitting on top of the gun. Of equal significance on the $1\frac{1}{2}$ Strutter was the installation of the rear Lewis gun. Although various kinds of mounting were tried, that which was to become standard equipment was of a new type designed by Warrant Officer Scarff of the Royal Naval Air Service. This mounting was in the form of a ring which encircled the gunner and which carried a movable arm, to which the gun was attached. So effective did the mounting prove that it was adopted not only by the British flying services but was later taken up by most of the air forces of the world, remaining in service until the Second World War.

The second of the Sopwith types was a single-seater which became known as the Pup. This name fitted it well, not only because of its lively powers of man-oeuvre, for which its light weight and small dimen-sions were largely responsible, but because its trim appearance proclaimed it as an offspring of the $1\frac{1}{2}$ Strutter. Never has an aeroplane been so unanimously acclaimed as 'the perfect flying machine'. One who has described it as such is Major Oliver Stewart, who was not only a distinguished RFC pilot of the Pup in combat but a test pilot also, and whose verdict is beyond question. Major Stewart said: 'In the Pup the pilots found that their speed was not high enough to be a predominant factor in combat. But the way the Pup climbed from, say, 8,000 ft upwards and the way it could cling to its height were proved to be of enormous value. The Pup could engage in circular chase tactics at 15,000 ft and keep circling without losing height, a thing of which no contemporary German aeroplane was capable.'

This expert opinion is an excellent illustration that speed is by no means the only requirement in a fighter; and certainly this was so in the frenzied whirl of the fighter-versus-fighter dogfights which developed in the period now under review. In the history of these combats the name of Richthofen is pre-eminent, and on 4 January 1917, this officer wrote in a combat report: 'One of the English aero-planes (Sopwith one-seater) attacked us and we saw immediately that the enemy aeroplane was superior to ours. Only because we were three against one, we detected the enemy's weak points. I managed to get behind him and shoot him down.'

But the nimble Pup could hardly change the course of the war, and, even as Richthofen wrote, the battle in the air was approaching a critical phase. The German fighter squadrons (Jagdstaffeln, or Jasta in brief) were strong and well equipped. They waited on their own side of the lines for the British and French reconnaissance machines, striking hard and often. In April 1917 casualties in the RFC were the highest of the war, the pilots and observer/gunners lost numbering 316. People called it Bloody April.

	Span	Length	Seats	Loaded weight	Maximum speed	Service ceiling	Armament
FRANCE							
Nieuport Baby	24′ 6″	19′ 0″	1	1,135 lb	102 mph	16,400 ft	1 r-c m-g
SPAD VII	25′ 8″	20′ 2″	1	1,664 lb	122 mph	18,400 ft	1 r-c m-g
GERMANY							
Albatros D.II	27′ 11″	24′ 3″	1	1,960 lb	109 mph	17,000 ft	2 r-c m-g
Fokker E.II	32′ 8″	23′ 2″	1	1,340 lb	87 mph	12,000 ft	1 r-c m-g
GREAT BRITAIN							
D.H.2	28′ 3″	25′ 2″	1	1,440 lb	93 mph	14,000 ft	1 r-c m-g
Sopwith 1½ Strutter	33′ 6″	25′ 3″	2	2,150 lb	100 mph	15,500 ft	2 r-c m-g
Sopwith Pup	26′ 6″	19′ 4″	1	1,225 lb	111 mph	17,500 ft	1 r-c m-g

3

First World War: The Tide of Battle Turns

In the grim April of 1917 the most famous fighters of the 1914–18 war were being designed, tested, or were already coming into service. The SPAD VII was doing excellent work with the French squadrons, setting a new standard of performance, as shown by the figures at the end of the last chapter, and improved versions of this fighter were to follow before the Armistice. Especially notable among these was the SPAD XII, which had a 37-mm cannon built in to the Hispano-Suiza water-cooled engine, the engine itself forming a rigid mounting and being known as a moteur canon, or engine cannon. The gun was of short-barrelled type and fired its shells through the hollow shaft which carried the airscrew. The breech, or rear end where the gun was loaded, was in the pilot's cockpit. Guynemer and Fonck, two of France's greatest aces (outstandingly successful

fighter pilots were so described), both achieved victories with this armament, but although the SPAD XII was built in considerable numbers it never achieved popularity, one reason being that the breech of the gun was uncomfortably close to the pilot and the explosive fumes dulled his senses. The principal replacement type for the SPAD VII was the SPAD XIII, with two Vickers machine-guns. Similarly armed was the Nieuport 28, used mainly by American squadrons.

One little-known and little-used SPAD biplane was the A4. This was an astonishing machine, with the fuselage or body in two sections, the airscrew revolving between them. The pilot was in the rear section and the gunner in a small separate open compartment out in the very front. For this reason a similar experimental British machine, the B.E.9, was

This SPAD XIII bears the insignia of France's famous 'Stork' squadron (*Les Cigognes*), of which Georges Guynemer, one of the greatest fighter pilots of all time, was a member.

called 'The Pulpit'. The name was appropriate for another reason, for an officer who was familiar with this strange aeroplane wrote: 'There was no communication possible between front and back seat; if anything happened, if the pilot were wounded, or even if nothing more serious occurred than a bad

landing in which the machine tipped over on its nose, the man in the box could but say his prayers: he would inevitably be crushed by the engine behind him.'

By the summer of 1917 new types of British fighter had made a name for themselves in combat with the best fighters the Germans could put into the air. These fighters were the Sopwith Triplane (three-winged, as the name denotes), the Sopwith Camel, the S.E.5a and the Bristol Fighter. The Triplane came as a very unpleasant surprise to the German pilots, although its Service career was brief. It was officially recorded that 'The sight of a Sopwith Triplane formation induced the enemy pilots to dive out of range,' and although the strange-looking British fighter when in action was likened to an 'intoxicated staircase' it was formidable indeed, largely by reason of its climbing powers. In manoeuvrability the type compared with the Pup, and this was partly due to the fitting of a rotary air-cooled engine. Being very compact, this type of engine enabled the fuselage to be made short in length, and, generally speaking, the smaller the fighter the greater its manoeuvrability. A short fuselage was one of the features of the Sopwith Camel biplane, so named because of the hump forward of the cockpit which housed the breech-casings of the two Vickers guns.

The Camel was probably the most manoeuvrable fighter ever built, both in a general and a particular sense. In general its handiness was due to small dimensions and the close grouping of the principal masses or weights, namely, engine, pilot, armament and fuel. In particular, by reason of the powerful torque, or twisting force, of its powerful rotary engine,

it turned far more swiftly to the right than to the left. It was a difficult aeroplane, but a deadly fighting machine. A Camel pilot was a man among men.

The Camel was a brilliant product of a private company, but the S.E.5a, with which it fought side by side in the last great battles of the war, was designed and first constructed by the Royal Aircraft Factory at Farnborough. One fighter pilot said of it after the Armistice: 'It came as near to "flying itself" as could be expected from a small machine with reasonably good control. Inevitably its stability diminished its controllability, and it was much less quick than a Camel, or to take a more truly comparable type, a SPAD. But its top speed was higher than that of the Camel, and those who liked it made great play with the theory that it provided a steady gun platform and that, in consequence, enemy aeroplanes could be engaged at greater ranges than they could from less stable but more sensitive machines.'

As may have been gathered, a stable aeroplane is one which, when disturbed from its normal flying attitude, returns to that attitude by itself. This quality, however, can be an enemy of manoeuvrability.

The armament for which the S.E.5a proved a steady platform was a fixed synchronised Vickers gun on the port (left) side of the fuselage and a Lewis

The horseshoe painted on the fuselage of this Sopwith Camel certainly brought the pilot luck, for the aircraft was in a mid-air collision with another, sustaining the damage seen.

gun on a track-type mounting over the top wing. This gun could fire straight ahead without being synchronised or it could be pulled down along the track for upward firing or the changing of ammunition magazines.

The last of the British machines at present under review, the two-seat Bristol Fighter, was first taken into service in the month before Bloody April, but

its full possibilities as a fighter were not discovered until later. This came about in a manner which shows very clearly the need to match fighting tactics to a particular aircraft. Before the circumstances are described the essential features of the aeroplane itself must be noted.

The Bristol Fighter provides a classic example of an aircraft designed round its armament, and in the

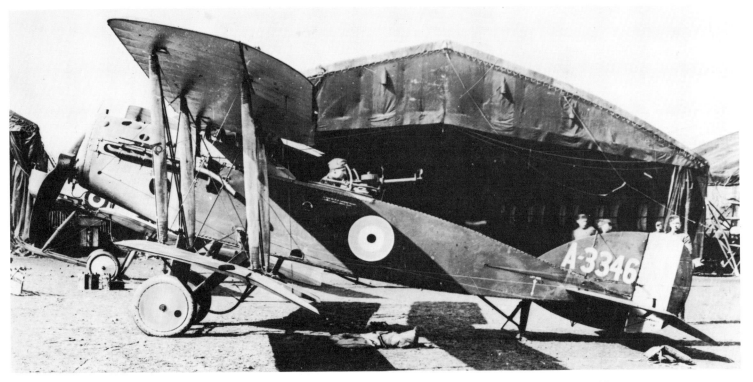

The Bristol Fighter was the most famous two-seater of its class during the 1914–18 war. This picture illustrates admirably the design features mentioned on the next page.

instance of the pilot's Vickers gun at least this was quite literally true. Having made up his mind to place this gun on the centreline of the aircraft the designer proceeded to do so, even though this necessitated making a tunnel through one of the petrol tanks. The only external evidence that a gun was indeed fitted was a small hole at the top of the radiator, where the bullets emerged, and the gunsights ahead of the pilot's cockpit. Two types of sight were installed together, following what had by this time become standard practice on British fighters. One sight was of simple ring-and-bead type, the other a tubular optical sight, embodying a system of lenses. This second type of sight, known as the Aldis sight, was not of the telescopic, or magnifying kind as often stated.

Although the Bristol Fighter's gunner normally had the same rear armament as on the earlier $1\frac{1}{2}$ Strutter (one Lewis gun on a Scarff ring-mounting) two guns were sometimes fitted, though these became somewhat difficult to handle at the heights now common for air combat, for the gunner quickly tired in the thin air. Also, the second gun added weight and air resistance, or drag. The most brilliant design features associated with the rear gun installation were to be seen in the layout of the aeroplane itself. First, the pilot and gunner were immediately next to each other, for easy communication. Then, of equal importance, the fuselage was set midway between the wings. This feature not only brought the pilot's eyes level with the top wing, allowing him the best possible view for fighting, but enabled the gunner to fire above the wing with relative ease. Of even greater importance to the gunner, the top line of the fuselage behind him was swept down, and the fin and rudder (the vertical surfaces for directional control of the aircraft) were disposed partly below the fuselage, thus allowing him a very wide field of fire.

These features have been described in some detail to illustrate how the disposition of armament and crew were very closely related to the design of the aeroplane itself, with the object of providing as nearly a perfect fighting machine as possible. Yet when the Bristol Fighter was first in action it met disaster, and it is this remarkable fact which illustrates the importance not only of good design but of correct fighting tactics also.

Five days before the Battle of Arras was due to start in April 1917 six of the first Bristol Fighters supplied to the RFC, led by Capt W. Leefe Robinson, VC, took part in an air offensive which opened along the entire British front line. They were attacked by six Albatros D.IIIs, led by Richthofen, and only two returned. One reason for this defeat was that the Fighters had been flown in the manner then usual for two-seaters, that is, as a firing platform for the gunner. Another reason was that the pilots mistakenly believed their new aircraft to be structurally weak and were reluctant to throw them about. Other defeats followed, but soon the pilots came to recognise that the main weapon of the Fighter was its fixed Vickers gun, and that they, and not the gunners, must take the offensive. This they did, and to such good effect that the Bristol Fighter soon became recognised as one of the truly great fighters of the 1914–18 war.

Mention of Leefe Robinson, VC, provides an occasion for recording how this officer earned his Victoria

Cross and also for turning to an aspect of fighter development that was essentially British. This concerned the attack of airships at night.

When, during 1915, the defence of Britain against night raids by airships was giving the Government much worry a type of aeroplane was selected for the task which differed very greatly indeed from the types of fighter then coming into being. This aeroplane, the B.E.2c, had been designed at the Royal Aircraft Factory as a very stable platform for reconnaissance, and when used for that purpose was to suffer very heavy casualties, partly by reason of its poor manoeuvrability. But the stability for which the B.E.2c was designed made it easy to fly by night, and the large area of the wings, in combination with quite a low weight, gave a low wing loading, or weight divided by wing area. This in turn gave low landing and take-off speeds, both desirable qualities in a night-flying fighter. Also with the destruction of airships in view, tests were made by the Royal Naval Air Service in the launching of B.E.2c aircraft from the gas bags of small airships. It was from aerodromes round London, however, that the B.Es were to gain their historic victories as fighting aeroplanes.

Their first attack was made on 31 March 1916, when 2nd-Lieut A. de B. Brandon caused the Zeppelin L.15 to alight on the sea by dropping upon it explosive darts and an incendiary bomb. These were typical of the curious weapons developed for the attack of airships. Grapnels, and rockets of a type invented by a French officer named Le Prieur, were carried; but it was the Lewis gun, firing special incendiary ammunition for setting fire to the gas in the airships, which enabled B.E.2cs to destroy four more of these monsters. The second of these was the Schütte-Lanz S.L.11, and for bringing this down, at Cuffley, north of London, Leefe Robinson was awarded his Victoria Cross.

Several later types of British aircraft were adapted for night fighting, using special gun installations, sometimes fixed and upward-firing, and necessitating flash eliminators, or devices for lessening the dazzling flash at the muzzles of the guns. Other devices were invented for illuminating the sights, and, experimentally, the target also, a searchlight being fitted in company with a type of rocket-firing gun. Developments such as these, however, were byproducts of the surging struggle for air supremacy, and the fighters of other nations now call for attention.

The German Albatros D.III 'vee-strutter', so known because of the form of its wing-bracing struts, had been introduced into service at about the same time as the Bristol Fighter, and, as already remarked, at first dealt severely with the British machine. With its two guns and good all-round performance it was one of the more successful fighters of the war, but its successors the D.V and D.Va showed insufficient improvement to regain from the Allies the command of the air which they were now winning.

July 1917 marked the beginning of replacement of Sopwith Triplanes by Camels; yet one month later the Germans themselves introduced a triplane, evidently inspired by, though by no means a copy of, the British single-seater. This was the Fokker Dr.I, the 'Dr.' signifying Dreidecker (triplane) just as E had denoted Eindecker (monoplane). Manoeuvrability and rate of climb were excellent, and the Dr.I was a favourite mount of the aces Richthofen and Voss. Richthofen's blood-red machine will always be remembered as the most vivid symbol of the German 'Flying Circuses', the large mobile formations of brightly and individually painted fighters. The Allied fighters were drab in comparison, the British machines commonly being a sort of olive green in colour. Between the wars, as later noted, they took on a much gayer appearance, but with the approach of the Second World War they were again put into battle dress to make them less conspicuous. The colours were then known as 'sand and spinach'.

The Fokker D.VII which followed the spectacular Dr.I was truly a masterpiece, and if this was not the finest fighter of the First World War, as is often claimed, then it was very high indeed on the list. This fighter was remarkable not only for its high

performance and ease of handling but for the form of its construction. Instead of being made of wood, as was usual at the time, the framework of the fuselage was made of steel tubes, as on the early Fokker monoplanes; but the wings were even more remarkable. These were of the cantilever type, meaning that they had no need for external bracing or steadying, the thin N struts between them being merely for the peace of mind of pilots who thought otherwise. In reality there was a third wing – a very small one through which the undercarriage axle passed.

Deadly fighter though it was (it was the only German fighter mentioned by name in the Armistice Agreement) the D.VII was, in respect of structure, a true forerunner of the famous Fokker airliners. Hardly less excellent, and also in service as the war neared its end, was the Pfalz D.XII. This had two sets of interplane, or between-wing, bracing struts on each side of the fuselage, and was thus of the two-bay biplane type. Several other fighters were of this type, including the F.E.2b, Bristol Fighter and Sopwith Snipe.

Having flown a D.VII with the lower wing removed altogether (an achievement which gave him much pleasure) Fokker produced the no less remarkable D.VIII monoplane. This was of parasol type, the wing being carried above the fuselage in the manner of an umbrella, whereas in the high-wing

The Fokker Dr.I triplane was of later design than the British ▶ Sopwith Triplane, which it strongly resembled. In a fighter of this type Manfred von Richthofen met his death.

The Fokker D.VII was in the forefront of the truly great fighters of 1914–18. As seen, the two machine-guns lay above the engine, which could be of Mercedes or BMW type.

type of monoplane the wing was attached directly to the top of the fuselage. The D.VIII came too late to influence the course of the war; and there were, in any case, German fighters of even more remarkable construction. These were of the Junkers all-metal low-wing type, with the corrugated, or wrinkled, sheet-metal covering which was to become familiar on the Junkers airliners between the wars. The first

(D.I) was a low-wing single-seater with a water-cooled engine and two guns; the second (CL.I) was a two-seater development of the same aircraft, designed to replace the Halberstadt CL types. These last-named biplanes had entered service in the summer of 1917 and were used not only for fighting but for the attack of ground targets. Recognising the importance of easy communication, the Halberstadt designers not only placed the pilot and gunner close together but arranged for them to share the same cockpit, the gun-ring being carried above the rear portion. Another two-seater in the same class was the very compact Hannover CL.II. The most distinctive feature of this aircraft was a biplane tail unit, designed to give the gunner the widest possible field of fire.

From the Vickers *Destroyer* of 1913 to the Boulton Paul Defiant of the Second World War, the two-seat fighter was continually challenging the ingenuity of designers in affording the gunner the least possible obstruction to his field of fire. How this was achieved on the Bristol Fighter and Hannover CL.II has been described. On the Junkers CL.I just mentioned the problem was eased by two features of design: first, there was no top wing to interfere; second, as the tail unit was of cantilever type there was no external bracing. Other types of German two-seat fighter displayed a different solution again. These were the

Hansa-Brandenburg W.12 and W.19 biplanes and W.29 and W.33 monoplanes, all of which were in service during the period now reviewed. On these fighters the rear fuselage was made very deep, to provide the required fin area, or side area, for directional stability and to enable the rudder to be mounted entirely below the top line of the fuselage. All these types were seaplanes, but although hampered by floats they gave a good account of themselves in air battles over the North Sea. In December 1917 a W.12 shot down the British airship C.27. There were frequent clashes with British flying-boats which, with their heavy armament, proved formidable opponents.

It may be noted here that as early as May 1916 a Bristol Scout had been launched experimentally from the top wing of a flying-boat, the object being to extend the Scout's endurance, or the time it could remain in the air, for anti-airship operations. Nearly a year earlier (3 November 1915) a Scout had taken-off from a flight deck built aboard the seaplane carrier HMS *Vindex*, and on 2 August 1917, a Sopwith Pup made the first successful landing aboard an aircraft carrier (HMS *Furious*) while the ship was steaming in the open sea. This historic landing said a great deal not only for the Pup's ease of handling, or controllability, but for the pilot's skill also, for the deck did not give a clear approach, as on later ships of the class, but lay ahead of a funnel and a massive superstructure, or structure built up from the deck. Pups were also flown from platforms aboard light cruisers, and one of these, from HMS *Yarmouth*, destroyed the Zeppelin L.23 on 21 August 1917. A special naval version of this tiny aeroplane, the Beardmore W.B.III, not only had folding wings, to make it easier to stow aboard naval vessels, but a folding undercarriage also, and may be considered as the first specialised carrier-borne fighter, or fighter specially designed to take-off from and land on the deck of an aircraft carrier.

Two types of specialised anti-airship fighter, neither of which progressed beyond the experimental stage, may be mentioned here to illustrate the amazing diversity of design apparent during the First World War. The first of these, the Grain Kitten, was designed to operate from small sea-going vessels with an armament of one Lewis gun. Having a wing span of only 18 ft this was certainly among the smallest fighters ever built, and with its two-cylinder 35 hp engine it weighed a mere 491 lb. At the other extreme was the Supermarine Night Hawk quadruplane (a number of experimental four-winged fighters were built) which measured 60 ft in span, weighed 6,146 lb and had two 100 hp engines. This monster carried a crew of three, who could man any of five positions, and the armament was one 2-pounder Davis recoil-less gun and three Lewis machine-guns. The Night Hawk was numbered among the experimental fighters which carried a searchlight, thereby antici-pating the Turbinlite fighters of the Second World War, which will later be mentioned.

A British fighter excluded from the earlier list of types which had distinguished themselves by the summer of 1917 was the D.H.5; yet although this type was undistinguished in combat, partly because of poor performance at altitude, it proved an admir-able machine for attacking ground targets. One factor in its success at this work was the excellence of the pilot's view, by virtue of the backward-staggered wings, the top wing being further back than the bottom wing. This same feature was reproduced in the Sopwith Dolphin, which entered service early in 1918. Unlike the D.H.5, the Dolphin had an excellent performance at height, and was armed not only with two Vickers guns but with two movable Lewis guns also, though these were often removed. The Dolphin had an Hispano-Suiza water-cooled engine, but the Snipe, a type of Sopwith fighter which was coming into service at the time of the Armistice, and was to be retained as a standard fighter of the Royal Air Force in later years, had a rotary engine. This engine, the Bentley B.R.2, was considerably more powerful (230 hp) than earlier engines of the rotary type and marked the practical limit of development along these lines. It will be shown how, in post-war years, the rivalry between the air-cooled and water-cooled or liquid-cooled engine was to continue; but the type of air-cooled engine then concerned was of the radial type, in which the cylinders radiated from the centre, as in the rotary engine, but which did not rotate. One such engine – the A.B.C. Dragonfly of 320 hp – was fitted experimentally in a Snipe before the war ended and gave a speed of 147·8 mph at 10,000 ft; but although ordered in great quantities for the Sopwith Dragon, Nieuport Nighthawk and other fine single-seaters, the Dragonfly proved a failure and these fighters never entered service.

One other type of British fighter which was never taken into service, although it was ordered in large numbers, was the Martinsyde Buzzard. This had a 300 hp Hispano-Suiza water-cooled engine and was nearly as fast as the experimental Snipe. Fighters were by this time becoming quite large and heavy, and the Buzzard had a wing span of 33 ft and weighed nearly 2,400 lb. Seeking to reverse this trend, the B.A.T. company built the tiny Bantam, which originally had a span of only 20 ft, though this was later increased to 25 ft, and which weighed little more than 1,300 lb. The Bantam was another promising British fighter which never entered service; but it was a true forerunner of the French *type jockey*

and the Folland Gnat, both later mentioned.

It has already been emphasised that speed is only one of several desirable qualities in a fighter, but this particular quality provides an impressive measure of fighter development during 1914–18 (remembering that a speed of 90 mph was considered high in 1914). Although having an engine of only 110 hp, and built as early as 1916, the Bristol Monoplane attained about 130 mph. The relatively poor view obtainable from the cockpit was a factor which led to its very limited use. The fastest fighters in production at the end of the war were the Martinsyde Buzzard and the Ansaldo S.V.A.5, a single-seater which marked the emergence of Italy as a leading manufacturer of fighters. The S.V.A.5 achieved 143 mph and retained an excellent performance even as a seaplane, being one of several types of 1914–18 fighters fitted with float undercarriage. It is fitting here to acknowledge also Italy's pioneering development of fighter flying-boats, one type (Macchi M.7) of 1918 having a speed of 130 mph. Hardly less creditable, for the aircraft concerned was a two-seater, was the speed of 133 mph recorded for the American Packard-Le Pere LUSAC-11. Two examples of this fighter were in France before the Armistice, giving notice that, as the fighter was now a well-established type, America was taking her place among the builders of such aircraft.

	Span	Length	Seats	Loaded weight	Maximum speed	Service ceiling	Armament
FRANCE							
SPAD XIII	26′ 6″	20′ 4″	1	1,862 lb	139 mph	21,800 ft	2 r-c m-g
GREAT BRITAIN							
Bristol Fighter	39′ 3″	25′ 10″	2	2,650 lb	123 mph	18,000 ft	2–3 r-c m-g
S.E.5a	26′ 7″	20′ 11″	1	2,048 lb	126 mph	17,000 ft	2 r-c m-g
Sopwith Triplane	26′ 6″	19′ 6″	1	1,415 lb	116 mph	20,000 ft	1 r-c m-g
Sopwith Camel	28′ 0″	18′ 9″	1	1,480 lb	120 mph	18,000 ft	2 r-c m-g
Sopwith Dolphin	32′ 6″	22′ 3″	1	2,000 lb	128 mph	21,000 ft	2–4 r-c m-g
Sopwith Snipe	31′ 1″	19′ 10″	1	2,020 lb	121 mph	19,500 ft	2 r-c m-g
GERMANY							
Albatros D.V	29′ 8″	24′ 0″	1	2,066 lb	116 mph	20,500 ft	2 r-c m-g
Fokker Dr.I	23′ 7″	18′ 11″	1	1,289 lb	103 mph	20,000 ft	2 r-c m-g
Fokker D.VII	29′ 2″	22′ 10″	1	1,985 lb	117 mph	19,680 ft	2 r-c m-g
Hannover CL.II	39′ 4″	25′ 5″	2	2,440 lb	103 mph	24,600 ft	2 r-c m-g
Hansa-Brandenburg W.33	52′ 0″	36′ 4″	2	4,510 lb	108 mph	16,000 ft	2–3 r-c m-g
Junkers D.I	29′ 6″	23′ 9″	1	1,840 lb	116 mph	19,680 ft	2 r-c m-g
Pfalz D.XII	29′ 6″	20′ 10″	1	1,980 lb	106 mph	18,500 ft	2 r-c m-g
ITALY							
Ansaldo S.V.A.5	29′ 10″	26′ 7″	1	2,315 lb	143 mph	19,680 ft	2 r-c m-g

4

Years of Peace: Netherlands, Germany, Great Britain, France

Between the two great wars the fighter became simpler in external appearance but far more complicated inside. Many designers were hesitant to depart from the biplane type, having regard to the favourable influence of its compactness and lightness on rate of climb and manoeuvrability. One illustration of this is afforded by the Hawker Fury biplane and the Hurricane monoplane: although the design of the former dated from the late 1920s, and the first Hurricane was not flown until late in 1935, the earlier machine took a slightly shorter time to climb to a height of 20,000 ft.

The trend towards the faster monoplane became inevitable, however, especially so as the bombers of the 1930s began to take advantage of precisely the same advances in design and engineering that were becoming available to the fighter itself. These included cantilever monoplane wings with higher wing loadings, made possible by devices for increasing the lifting power of the wing at low speeds (high-lift devices); retractable undercarriages, enclosed cockpits and smooth metal coverings, or skins, to give further reductions in drag and increases in speed; engines delivering more power, especially at high altitudes, by virtue of superchargers, which forced more air or fuel/air mixture into an engine than it could otherwise take in; and variable-pitch air-screws, which, by having the angle of their blades varied, could make more effective use of the power available. These advances themselves meant greater complication and weight, and even more weight was added by the increasing amount of equipment and armament demanded.

Even as the First World War had neared its end combats were taking place at heights of about 20,000 ft (on 11 August 1918, a Camel, flown from a lighter, or flat-decked craft, towed behind a destroyer, shot down Zeppelin L.53 at 19,000 ft), and oxygen equipment had then become necessary to maintain a pilot's efficiency in the thin air. It was needful also to heat not only the pilot's clothing but the guns as well, to prevent the lubricating oil from freezing. Then came demands for radio equipment, increasing still further the effectiveness of the fighters of the 1920s and 1930s, but increasing also weight, complication and demands on the pilot. Following wartime practice, provision was often made for bombs for the attack of ground targets, and by the early 1920s a parachute had been added to the pilot's personal apparel – a merciful but cumbersome innovation.

As the period now reviewed neared its end there was a sharp general increase in the weight of armament, and this was accompanied by new forms of gun-firing gear, the guns often being mounted in the wings outboard of the airscrew, so that no synchron-

ising gear was required. At the same time a gunsight of the reflector type was adopted. In this type of sight, the sighting graticule, or pattern of rings and lines, was projected on to a glass reflector by means of an electric light, the brightness of which could be controlled. Unlike earlier sights this was installed in the cockpit. Although night-flying gear in the form of special lighting had been carried by certain fighters before 1918 this was now more common, for darkness had become a favourite defence for the bomber. For naval carrier-borne fighters yet other items of equipment were now required. These included arrester gear, usually in the form of a hook which could be lowered at landing to pick up wires on the deck of the carrier, thus bringing the fighter quickly to a standstill; fittings on the fuselage enabling it to be catapulted into the air; air bags allowing it to float in case of a forced descent in the sea; a dinghy and markers to improve the pilot's chances of survival – and slinging gear for use in salvage operations!

The designer of a naval fighter was a thoughtful man indeed.

As though all these requirements were not enough, the addition of armour-plate protection for the pilot and other vulnerable items was demanded just before war came; and even this was insufficient, for a bullet-proof windscreen became a further must. Small wonder, with fighters now so fast, large and heavy, that people declared that the day of the dogfight was over. Not so: the coming war showed that all that was needed was more sky room in which to manoeuvre.

The major trends outlined were of a general nature and there were some interesting exceptions, calling for mention as the inter-war fighters of several nations are reviewed. It will later be gathered that the period was rich in variety, although development was often affected by financial considerations. For the same reason, much equipment and armament of a type developed during 1914–18 was retained. The period was, nevertheless, a colourful one, not only in the sense of wide variety but because the machines themselves were usually gay with national and other markings. The Royal Air Force, in particular, gave its fighters a dazzling collection of colour schemes. These were not merely for decoration but to distinguish the various squadrons in the air, recalling the ancient days of chivalry and heraldry. Small streamers, or pennants, were flown on British fighters to distinguish a squadron leader's or a flight leader's aircraft, a flight being a component part – usually one third – of a squadron of nine aircraft. As speeds increased, however, the pennants were torn to shreds, and, quite literally, were no more seen.

This Fokker D.XVI has a British Armstrong Siddeley Jaguar engine and displays the mainly red, white and blue markings of the Netherlands. The small central disc is orange.

This was the period also when aerobatic evolutions, even by large formations, became popular public spectacles; but it was the period likewise of the Spanish Civil War, involving German, Italian and Soviet fighters in a grim contest, foreshadowing the world-wide struggle to come. Some of the fighters engaged were, in fact, among the first to be built in Germany since the days of the Fokker D.VII.

Anthony Fokker's company continued to build fighters in the Netherlands, and the D.XVI and

D.XVII, in service in the early 1930s, bore a certain family resemblance to that excellent aircraft, although the wings were tapered and not constant in chord (distance from leading edge to trailing edge). The D.XXI of 1936 was a low-wing cantilever monoplane with non-retractable undercarriage, and this type, like the G.I later mentioned, was in action against the invading Germans. Other D.XXIs were flown by Finnish pilots against the Russians.

When the new German Air Force was formed in 1933 two types of single-seater were chosen for production, both biplanes and both of mixed (wood and metal) construction. These were the Heinkel He 51 and the Arado Ar 68, the former serving, without great distinction, in Spain. A later type, a monoplane of very great distinction indeed, was the Messerschmitt Me 109 (sometimes written Bf 109), first flown in 1935 with a British Rolls-Royce Kestrel engine. In various developed forms this was to remain a standard fighter throughout the Second World War and was to equip a number of other air forces until the mid-1960s. The first model to go into service was the Me 109B, which had the new Junkers Jumo 210 inverted-vee engine (so described because of its shape as viewed end-on), and was armed with either three machine-guns or two guns of this type and a 20-mm cannon. This excellent fighter achieved success in Spain and was further developed with

increased armament and more powerful Daimler-Benz engines, also of inverted-vee type. The chief developments will be described in the following chapter, together with the twin-engined Me 110, first flown in 1936.

The Me 109 thus appeared at about the same time as Britain's Hawker Hurricane and Supermarine Spitfire, which, as the Me 109E, it was to meet in the fateful combats of the Battle of Britain. The two British types had been preceded in Royal Air Force service by the Gloster Grebe, Hawker Woodcock, Armstrong Whitworth Siskin, Gloster Gamecock, Bristol Bulldog, Hawker Fury and Demon and Gloster Gauntlet and Gladiator. All of these were biplanes, with the exception of the Siskin, which was a sesquiplane or one-and-a-half-winger. The Siskin, in its Mark III form, had the further distinction of being the first fighter of metal construction (in this case steel) to enter RAF service. The covering, however, was still largely of fabric, and the first RAF fighter to have a metal skin as well as a metal framework, was the Spitfire. The Siskin was also notable, in its Mark IIIA form, as the first RAF fighter to have a supercharged engine (Armstrong Siddeley Jaguar). The Gamecock was often described as 'the RAF's last wooden fighter'; and so it was – until the arrival of 'The Wooden Wonder', or de Havilland Mosquito, many years later.

The black-and-white chequered markings denote that these ▶
Armstrong Whitworth Siskins belong to the RAF's No 43
Squadron. They are joined by elastic ropes to demonstrate
precise flying.

A smart turn-out by the Gloster Gamecocks of No 23 Squadron, RAF. The squadron markings were alternate squares of red and blue, and the squadron commander's aircraft (nearest) carried them not only on the top wing and fuselage sides but on top of the fuselage also.

With the exception of the Fury and Demon all the types named had an air-cooled engine of either Armstrong Siddeley or Bristol type; and all except the Demon and Gladiator were armed with two Vickers guns only, thus being hardly more formidable in firepower than the Camel of the First World War and definitely inferior to the Dolphin. Although in 1932 a predecessor of the Gauntlet (S.S.19) had been fitted experimentally with four Lewis guns in addition to the two normal Vickers guns, receiving wide publicity on that account, this multi-gun armament was virtually identical with that secretly installed on the Sopwith Snark experimental triplane of 1918.

On the Hurricane and Spitfire one of the most massive advances in fighter armament was made at a single step: no fewer than eight rifle-calibre machine-guns were installed in the wings outboard of the airscrew. These guns were of the excellent American Browning type, adopted by the RAF in succession to the Vickers; and a remarkable fact which appears to have eluded the aeronautical historians is that an earlier model of the Browning gun had been experimentally installed on an RAF Bristol Fighter as long before as 1918. Even heavier armament for the two British monoplanes will be referred to later: meanwhile further mention must be made of the Fury, Demon and Gladiator, for each was distinctive.

As British cities, and in particular London, were

quite close to the sea, and as the speed and height capabilities of bombers were constantly increasing, it was recognised that very little warning of enemy raids would be possible. An extremely high rate of climb was therefore a first requirement for a new class of intercepter fighter, which materialised in RAF squadrons as the Fury. Even radio and night-flying gear were dispensed with in the interests of lightness, and not only was the Fury able to climb to 20,000 ft in about $9\frac{1}{2}$ min (the contemporary Bulldog took 15 min or more), but it was the first fighter in service capable of over 200 mph.

The Demon was significant because it was the first two-seat fighter to be used by the RAF since the Bristol Fighter and because, in its later form, it was fitted with a power-driven gun turret, which enabled the gunner to aim his Lewis gun without effort at high speeds and great heights. This turret was a very remarkable device indeed, and was described as being of lobster-back type. This meant that the curved metal shield which protected the gunner from the rush of air was made in sections which fitted one over the other. After testing the turret in the air, while the driving mechanism was still on the Secret List, the present writer reported: 'It is the most human gadget imaginable; one has only to think of the direction in which one wishes to aim the gun and the indescribable mechanism seems to do the

rest.' The Gladiator's armament was less remarkable but quite significant, for in addition to two Browning guns in the fuselage there were two others in the wings.

Revival of the two-seat fighter, and the fitting of the turret on the Demon, led to a totally new (if, as will later be seen, misguided) departure in fighter design. This was the turret fighter, in which the entire armament was concentrated in the turret, the pilot being concerned only with placing the aircraft in the best position relative to the target. This idea materialised as the Boulton Paul Defiant, first flown in 1937. Being powered with the Rolls-Royce Merlin, as were the Spitfire and Hurricane, and having automatically retractable fairings, or streamlined casings, in front of and behind the turret, the Defiant had a good performance, but was inevitably slower and less manoeuvrable than the single-seaters. What befell the Defiant in battle will later be described.

For service in aircraft carriers Britain took into service in the 1920s the sturdy little Fairey Flycatcher. This was succeeded in the early 1930s by the Hawker Nimrod (a larger development of the Fury) and, in 1939, by the Gloster Sea Gladiator. The Hawker Osprey was a naval counterpart of the Demon, but was intended for reconnaissance as well as fighting and had only one fixed gun instead of two; and the Blackburn Roc was a turret fighter like the Defiant,

The Fairey Flycatcher was a fascinating little fighter, whether mounted on wheels or floats. This amphibious specimen has both, the wheels being set in the floats.

but of even lower performance. A companion Blackburn type in service was the Skua, which was a dive-bomber as well as a fighter but carried four fixed guns and one free gun. A Skua was the first British fighter to shoot down an enemy aircraft in the Second World War.

Experimental British fighters in the years between the wars included two unusual classes, one a single-engined single-seater, the other a three-seater with two engines. These were designed to attack bombers

from below with upward-firing guns, and examples were built by the Westland, Vickers and Bristol companies. The single-seaters had a 37-mm cannon made by the Coventry Ordnance Works (and consequently known as the Cow gun) fixed to the starboard, or right-hand, side of the fuselage; the three-seater carried two such guns, one fixed and upward-firing, the other on a rotatable ring-mounting which allowed also elevation and depression. It was in France, however, that cannon armament was chiefly developed, and to the fighters of that nation attention is now turned.

The famous name of Nieuport was one that continued to be borne for several years by French single-seaters. Though the Nieuport 29 was a biplane, the Nieuport-Delage 42, 52 and 62 were sesquiplanes. Together with the Loire-Gourdou-Leseurre 32 and Wibault 72 parasol monoplanes, various models of the Type 62 formed the basic equipment of the French fighter squadrons for a lengthy period. The Wibault 72 was especially notable for its strong metal structure, for which the Vickers company in Great Britain acquired manufacturing rights. Two or four machine-guns were fitted, and the type was further developed for operation from aircraft carriers.

A second famous name – that of SPAD – was continued over a number of years by a series of biplanes bearing the type numbers XX, 61, 81 and

510. The first SPAD XX had been flown before the Armistice and was remarkable for the cleanness of its design (there was only one interplane bracing strut on each side) and in being a two-seater with a moteur canon. On production examples, however, two machine-guns were fitted instead, and the cannon was not to reappear on French fighters until the 1930s. The last of the SPADs, the 510, was in some ways comparable with Britain's Gloster Gladiator and had a similar armament of four machine-guns.

Yet a third name associated with fighters of 1914–18 was that of Morane-Saulnier, and this was connected in the 1930s with the compact and attractive-looking M-S 225, widely acclaimed for its aerobatic performances by a squadron known as the Patrouille de Dijon (Dijon Patrol). The M-S 225 was a parasol monoplane, but the M-S 406, the best known French fighter of the 1939–45 war, was a low-wing type, like its British counterparts the Hurricane and Spitfire. Though armed with a 20-mm cannon and two machine-guns it was inferior in performance to the British machines and also to the Me 109 which opposed it in the early months of war.

The Hispano-Suiza engine cannon of the type fitted to the M-S 406, and which recalled the SPAD XII of 1917–18, had been reintroduced into French fighter squadrons on fighters of the Dewoitine D.500 series. The low-wing D.500 had been preceded by several parasol-wing Dewoitine single-seaters, the last of which were of the D.37 series. Some of these fighters had two 20-mm cannon, mounted in the wings; others had four machine-guns. One version was supplied to the French Navy as a replacement for its carrier-borne Wibaults.

The Dewoitine D.37 series marked the final development of the parasol monoplane fighter in France, for, as already noted, the D.500 series fighters were of low-wing type. One great advantage of this type was that it enabled the wheels to be retracted relatively easily into the wing, but on the D.500s the undercarriage was of fixed type, with streamlined casings over the wheels. It was the revived moteur canon armament of the D.501 which attracted the greatest attention abroad, and examples of this fighter were acquired for study by both Great Britain and the USSR. The gun concerned differed very greatly from the type employed in combat by Guynemer and Fonck. The calibre (20 mm) was smaller, but the shells were fired automatically, instead of singly, and the speed and accuracy with which they were delivered were far higher by reason of the long barrel. Guns of this general type were later to be made in Britain, becoming known by the name British Hispano and being fitted to many types of fighter.

A development of the D.500 series was the D.520, which had a retractable undercarriage and was used, alongside the M-S 406, in the Battle of France. A remarkable story can be told of the D.520 concerning engines and guns. Owing to difficulties in the supply of Hispano-Suiza engines a version of the aircraft was arranged to take the British Rolls-Royce Merlin. This engine had not been designed for the mounting of a cannon, so provision was made for installing two such guns in the wings, thereby anticipating the later versions of the Spitfire and Hurricane, with their wing-mounted British-Hispano armament.

In fairness to British designers, however, it must be recorded that a cannon-armed version of the Hurricane had been proposed as early as February 1936 and that an experimental installation in the wing of a Hurricane had been made in the spring of 1939. True, the Dewoitine D.37 series and other similar fighters had wing-mounted cannon even earlier; but the structural stiffness of the wings of the period lacked the rigidity desirable for the most effective use of cannon, and this was one reason why the moteur canon was generally preferred.

The moteur canon was distinctively French: so, also, was the *type jockey*. As the term suggests, this was a type of lightweight fighter, and those who favoured it emphasised its cheapness and ease of manufacture. A number of examples were built, but

these were more or less experimental, and the first to receive a sizable production order was the Caudron C.714. Just as the Spitfire gained from its designer's experience with seaplanes built for the Schneider Trophy contests, so did the French fighter reproduce features of previous Caudron racers, designed to attain the highest possible speed with the smallest possible engine. The 450 hp Renault air-cooled engine of the C.714 was, indeed, only about half as powerful as types generally being installed in fighters of the period, but nevertheless a speed of slightly over 300 mph was achieved. C.714s were flown in action by Polish pilots.

Curiously enough, France had an inclination not only toward the light fighter but to the heavy fighter also and constructed a number of machines described as multiplace de combat, or multi-seat battleplane. These were real flying fortresses, twin-engined and bristling with guns; but although fighting was supposedly included among their duties they were essentially bombers. They were, incidentally, among the ugliest aeroplanes ever built and brought little credit to France in any way. One such aeroplane had been built by the Breguet company, but was never put into production. There was, however, a notable Breguet twin-engined fighter/bomber which resulted from a French Air Staff requirement of 1934, calling for a specialised twin-engined fighter. Breguet

The Morane-Saulnier M-S 406 was the most famous French fighter of the Second World War.
The radio aerial seen beneath the fuselage retracted when the wheels were extended.

decided to build a machine suitable for other duties also, and their 690 series was the outcome. The specialised fighter version was the 697, which promised very high performance indeed, but the only example built was deliberately destroyed in 1940 to prevent it from falling into German hands. One type which originated from the same requirement, and which actually equipped French fighter units, was the Potez 631, which eventually had a forward-firing armament of two 20-mm cannon and six machine-guns and two free machine-guns for the gunner. This fighter greatly resembled the opposing Messerschmitt Me 110, but having engines of lower power was inferior in performance.

When Germany attacked France in May 1940 many French fighter squadrons were equipped with Bloch MB-151 and 152 single-engined fighters, sound in design and construction but inferior to their British and German counterparts. Comparable fighters in French service were American Curtiss Hawk monoplanes, and the development of these and other American fighters is described in the next chapter.

	Span	Length	Seats	Loaded weight	Maximum speed	Service ceiling	Armament
GERMANY							
Heinkel He 51	36′ 1″	27′ 7″	1	4,180 lb	205 mph	25,350 ft	2 r-c m-g
Messerschmitt Me 109B	32′ 4″	28′ 4″	1	4,805 lb	292 mph	26,570 ft	3 r-c m-g
GREAT BRITAIN							
Armstrong Whitworth Siskin IIIA	33′ 2″	25′ 4″	1	3,232 lb	145 mph	27,000 ft	2 r-c m-g
Bristol Bulldog IIA	33′ 10″	24′ 9″	1	3,529 lb	163 mph	27,000 ft	2 r-c m-g
Gloster Gamecock	29′ 9″	19′ 8″	1	2,863 lb	155 mph	22,000 ft	2 r-c m-g
Hawker Fury	30′ 0″	26′ 8″	1	3,490 lb	207 mph	28,000 ft	2 r-c m-g
Hawker Demon	37′ 3″	29′ 7″	2	4,668 lb	182 mph	27,500 ft	3 r-c m-g
Gloster Gladiator	32′ 3″	27′ 5″	1	4,750 lb	253 mph	33,000 ft	4 r-c m-g
FRANCE							
Wibault 72	36′ 0″	24′ 9″	1	3,350 lb	156 mph	27,900 ft	2 or 4 r-c m-g
Dewoitine D.501	39′ 8″	25′ 3″	1	3,790 lb	224 mph	35,400 ft	1 c+2 r-c m-g
Morane-Saulnier M-S 406	35′ 1″	26′ 10″	1	5,445 lb	305 mph	32,300 ft	1 c+2 r-c m-g
Potez 631	52′ 6″	36′ 4″	2	8,230 lb	276 mph	32,800 ft	2 c+7 r-c m-g

5

Years of Peace: USA, Italy, USSR, Japan

The first single-seat fighter of United States design and construction to be taken into service was the Thomas Morse MB-3A, a machine designed in 1918 to surpass the SPAD VII then used by American squadrons. Hardly surprisingly, there were points of resemblance to the excellent French fighter. For the greater part of the 1920s and '30s, however, American fighter design was largely in the hands of the Curtiss and Boeing companies. Curtiss had originally been chosen to build British-designed S.E.5a fighters, but completed only one. The company then secured a production contract for a fighter design by the Army Engineering Division and somewhat resembling the MB-3A. This became known as the Curtiss/Orenco Model D and was historically notable because it was fitted experimentally with an exhaust-driven turbo-supercharger.

This type of supercharger is driven by a gas-turbine wheel turned by the exhaust gases from the engine, instead of being driven mechanically as in the more common type, and superchargers of this sort were widely used on American fighters of the Second World War. The next Curtiss type also had a particular interest, having been designed at the Naval Aircraft Factory for service aboard America's first aircraft carrier, the USS *Langley*. A light, low-powered biplane, it was armed with one machine-gun. The first all-Curtiss fighter was the PW-8, which quickly distinguished itself by making the first dawn-to-dusk flight across the North American continent. A notable design feature was the type of radiator, which formed part of the wing surface, contributing (by reducing drag) to the excellent top speed of 165 mph. The armament of one rifle-calibre (0·30 in) machine-gun and one heavy machine-gun (0·50 in) was to become common on American fighters for many years to come.

The first fighter of the US Air Force's famous P (pursuit) series, which continued until 1948, when the P was changed to F for fighter, was the Curtiss P-1 Hawk. This was known in the US Navy as the F6C, the term fighter having been favoured by the US Navy from the earliest days. The C signified Curtiss, for the Navy believed in giving credit to the manufacturer concerned. As used by the US Army Air Corps (as it then was), the P-1 had the Curtiss D-12 water-cooled engine, which was remarkable for its small head resistance or frontal area; but the US Navy preferred an air-cooled radial engine, and some F6C-4s so powered were put into service. The F7C-1 was designed from the outset as a carrier-borne fighter. With the P-6 Hawk series came an engine-cooling system using ethylene glycol instead of water and enabling the radiator for the Curtiss Conqueror engine to be made smaller. As its designation implies, the F8C was a fighter (actually a two-seater with four guns); but it was as a dive-bomber – the famous Helldiver round which a film was made – that this type achieved its greatest renown.

The F9C Sparrowhawk was another historic Curtiss type, being designed as a parasite fighter to be carried by, and launched from, the airships *Akron* and *Macon*. These fighters could hook-on to the mother ship by means of a massive attachment carried above the fuselage. In the design of the F11C single-seater the ability to make dive-bombing attacks was again accentuated, and the later aircraft of the series were remarkable in having a retractable undercarriage. Not only did this feature lessen drag in the air but it made the aircraft easier to ditch, or put down in the sea in emergency. With a fixed undercarriage there was a danger of overturning when the aircraft tripped over its own undercarriage. The undercarriage of the F11C retracted into the sides of the fuselage, but when low-wing cantilever monoplanes came into general use it was usual to retract the undercarriage into the wing. One such monoplane having this feature was the Curtiss P-36, for export versions of which the name Hawk was revived, as already noted in connection with the French Air Force. Of the handling qualities of the Hawk 75, as supplied to France, an experienced test pilot has said: 'Although performance of the Hawk 75 was not in the same street as that of the Spitfire, comparative trials revealed that its beautifully harmonised controls made it far superior, with ability to manoeuvre more quickly and accurately in a dive owing to its very light ailerons, and better in a dogfight because the elevators were not over-

The Curtiss F9C-2 Sparrowhawk had two hooks. The one above ▶ the fuselage was for hooking-on to an airship while that attached under the tail was for engaging the arrester wires of an aircraft carrier.

sensitive like those of the Spitfire – the controls of which, despite popular opinion, were poor . . .' (Ailerons control rolling movement, elevators control climb and dive.)

Another radial-engined American fighter, with undercarriage retracting into the fuselage instead of into the wing as on the Hawk, was the Brewster F2A Buffalo, originally developed for the US Navy but also exported in considerable numbers. This was neither a biplane nor a low-wing monoplane, the cantilever wing being attached at roughly the middle of the fuselage; but although displaying a number of unusual features of design this stubby little fighter proved distinctly inferior to its Japanese opponents.

Of the Boeing fighters, the first in service was the PW-9 (US Navy FB-1), notable for its tapered biplane wings and the radiator mounted in a tunnel under the Curtiss water-cooled engine. The F2B and F3B were developments for the US Navy, with air-cooled engines. Most famous of all the Boeing biplane fighters was the P-12, known as F4B in the Navy and Model 100 in the export market. The stubby appearance of these fascinating little fighters was accentuated by the comparatively large diameter of the Pratt & Whitney Wasp radial engine, later surrounded by a drag-reducing ring, and another very distinctive feature of later versions was the massive headrest behind the cockpit. An even more

prominent headrest appeared on Boeing's first monoplane fighter, the P-26, which entered service in 1933/34; and the striking appearance of this fighter was heightened by the fact that the low-set wing was externally braced by wires attached to the fuselage and to the fixed undercarriage. The vertical legs of the undercarriage were covered by large fairings, or streamlined casings, which soon became known as trousers, or pants. This last description was also used in America to describe the streamlined casings fitted over the wheels themselves, and which were also a feature of the P-26. In England these were called spats.

Technically, the P-26 had an even greater interest, for in its original form it had no hinged flaps on the trailing edge, or rear portion, of the wing. These were later fitted, and flaps then became normal equipment on monoplane fighters of the late 1930s. Their purpose was to increase the lift of the wing, or the lift and drag combined, and they are not to be confused with the air brakes which later became normal equipment on jet fighters. The sole purpose of these was to increase drag.

The P-26 was the last Boeing fighter to enter service. Flown by pilots of the Philippine Army, fighters of this type were in action at Pearl Harbor in 1941.

One of the truly great fighters of the war in the Pacific and in Europe, the Republic P-47 Thunder-

Although it entered service as early as 1933 the Boeing P-26 was in action at Pearl Harbor during 1941.
Fighters of this type had by that time been handed over to the Philippine Army.

bolt, traced its ancestry to the Seversky P-35, first built in 1935 and supplied in some numbers to the USAAC. Two examples of a related two-seater type were supplied to Russia. Even more strongly resembling the Thunderbolt was the Republic P-43 Lancer, the name of the makers having been changed at a time of reorganisation.

Two other great fighters of the war which came in 1939, the Grumman Wildcat and Hellcat, were descended from the US Navy's Grumman FF-1 of 1931. This attracted great attention at the time because, although a biplane, it had a retractable undercarriage, the wheels folding into the sides of the fuselage as on the later Curtiss F11C. When the first FF-1 was tested late in 1931 it attained a speed of 195 mph. It is sometimes stated that this speed was higher than that achieved by any single-seater then in service; but this is incorrect, for the Hawker Fury, then serving with the RAF, had a speed of 207 mph. The FF-1 was nevertheless remarkable, for it was a two-seater; nor was it the only American fighter of this class to be taken into service, as will be noted later.

Design features of the FF-1 were reproduced in the F2F and F3F single-seaters, the latter being especially remarkable in appearance by reason of the large diameter of the Wright Cyclone radial engine, which made the front of the fuselage very fat. The earlier, and more attractive-looking, F2F had a Pratt & Whitney Twin Wasp Junior engine of two-row type. This meant that, instead of having nine large cylinders in a single row like the Cyclone it had fourteen smaller cylinders arranged in two rows and having a noticeably smaller diameter.

A larger and more powerful type of Pratt & Whitney two-row engine, the Twin Wasp, was installed in the F4F Wildcat, the first of the Grumman monoplanes and the last of the Grumman fighters to have the type of undercarriage fitted to the FF-1. Further reference to this fighter will be made in the following chapter; meanwhile the present review of American fighters may be concluded by noting the characteristics of two types of two-seat fighter which served in American squadrons in addition to the Grumman FF-1. The first of these was the Berliner-Joyce P-16 of 1929, later known as the PB-1. This biplane could almost be classed as a sesquiplane, for the top wing was much larger than the lower wing; but the most remarkable feature was the way in which the roots, or innermost sections, of the top wing were tilted down for attachment to the fuselage. The object of this arrangement – known as the gull wing – was to improve the pilot's view. The second two-seater was a remarkable aircraft in many respects. This was the Consolidated P-30 (later PB-2) monoplane with turbo-supercharged Curtiss Conqueror engine cooled by ethylene glycol. Not the least remarkable fact concerning this fighter is that it was developed from a commercial machine known as the Lockheed Altair. A speed of 239 mph was attained, and it is said that the difficulty experienced by the gunner in aiming his gun at speeds of this order led to America's abandonment of the two-seat fighter. This may well have been so; but it must be remarked that a similar type of free-gun installation – without power assistance for the gunner – was retained on later and much faster two-seat fighters, notably the German Me 110.

In Chapter 3 it was remarked that one of the fastest fighters of the 1914–18 war was the Italian Ansaldo S.V.A.5; yet manoeuvrability, rather than speed, was stressed by Italian designers between the wars. The most famous of Italy's fighters were the biplanes made by the Fiat company, and the first of these, the C.R.1, had a peculiar zig-zag arrangement of bracing struts between the wings, an arrangement which, in its general form, was to be retained throughout the series. Even more remarkable, the top wing was smaller than the bottom wing, whereas the reverse was true of other fighters with wings of unequal span, and these included the later C.R.20. The C.R.30 was notably cleaner in design, with a view to reducing drag and increasing speed; and generally similar, though somewhat smaller, was the most famous Fiat fighter of all, the C.R.32 which took part in quite astonishing aerobatic displays and equipped *La Cucaracha* squadron in the Spanish Civil War. The Fiat C.R.42 – the last type in the series – was not put into production until a few months before war came. It differed from its predecessors in having an air-cooled engine and, although at first armed with one rifle-calibre and one heavy machine-gun (a practice followed by Italy as well as the USA) it was adapted as the war progressed to take four of the heavy guns. C.R.42s escorted bombing raids on England, and the manoeuvrability of a captured two-gun specimen was described by RAF pilots in the most enthusiastic terms. A Fiat monoplane, the G.50, saw service both in the Spanish Civil War and in the greater war to follow, and this, too, was noted for its manoeuvring powers. Generally similar in design, though slightly faster, were the Macchi C.200 and Caproni-Vizzola F.5.

Many nations were building fighters between the wars, and the Polish gull-wing P.Z.L. series and the Dutch twin-boom Fokker G.I will later receive special mention. The present account, however, must be concluded with an outline of Russian and Japanese developments.

Two Russian biplane fighters were built during the First World War to the designs of Igor Sikorsky, and the Moscow Aviation Works produced mono-plane types known as the Mosca MB and MB bis (second). In the 1920s there were the Junkers parasol-wing H-21 two-seater, Polikarpov I-1 low-wing single-seater and Tupolev I-4 single-seat sesquiplane, two of which were carried above the wing of a large bomber, recalling the wartime experiment with a Bristol Scout.

The first Russian-designed fighter to be built in considerable numbers was the Grigorovich I-2, a feature of which was a plywood-covered fuselage. This was a feature also of Soviet fighters of much later design.

The 1930s saw production of more new Soviet fighters – single-seat biplanes and monoplanes of very remarkable design indeed. The biplanes were the Polikarpov-Grigorovitch I-5 and the Polikarpov I-15, the latter having a top wing of gull form, already mentioned in connection with the Berliner-Joyce two-seater and the Polish P.Z.L. series. This feature was abandoned on the I-15 bis but was again adopted for the I-153, the most remarkable feature of which was a retractable undercarriage. This retracted not into the fuselage sides, as on American Grumman and Curtiss fighter biplanes already mentioned, but lay in wells in the bottom of the fuselage and lower wing roots. When fighting broke out in Mongolia during 1939 the I-153 proved superior to the Japanese Nakajimi Ki-27 monoplane later mentioned. The sight of biplanes with retractable undercarriages fighting monoplanes with fixed undercarriages must have been a memorable one indeed. Likewise memorable, for Western observers at least, would have been the spectacle of Soviet fighters of the types mentioned taking-off and landing on skis, which they frequently did.

The Polikarpov monoplanes were the I-16, with air-cooled radial engine, and the I-17, with water-cooled engine. When it entered service in 1934 the squat little I-16 was certainly among the world's finest fighters and was in some ways a match for the

Over typical Russian terrain these two stubby little Polikarpov I-16s are seen in 'open', or 'loose', formation. The humps housing the machine-guns are seen ahead of the cockpit.

early Me 109s in the Spanish Civil War. In 1939 fighters of this type used rockets to attack Japanese aircraft and forces on the ground, recalling the Le Prieur rockets of 1914–18 and foreshadowing the guided missiles which were to arm the fighters of coming years.

Another unusual form of armament may be mentioned in connection with the Grigorovitch PI-1, a little-known low-wing single-seater, small numbers of which entered service in 1934. This carried two

75-mm recoilless guns, of a general type fitted experimentally on British aircraft during 1914–18. The Russian fighter was not a success, partly because of low rate of fire.

That the first fighter built in Japan – the carrier-borne Mitsubishi 1MF1 biplane – should have borne a resemblance to the experimental Sopwith Snapper is explained by the fact that both aircraft were designed by the Englishman Herbert Smith. Mitsubishi's next fighter, however, was of distinctly original design. This was the A5M, a low-wing monoplane with fixed undercarriage, first flown in 1935. At this time enclosed cockpits were becoming fashionable for fighters, but Japanese A5M pilots objected to being shut in and this type of fighter was one of the last to go into action roofless. One A5M successfully returned from combat with two thirds of its port wing missing. Two biplane fighters of

Japanese design were the Kawasaki Type 92 of 1930 and the Ki-10 built some five years later. The third name associated with fighters was Nakajima. The A1N was the British Gloster Gambet built under licence, but the A2N was a very successful original design. The Nakajima Type 91 was a parasol monoplane, the A4N1 another biplane, and the Ki-27 a low-wing monoplane somewhat resembling the A5M but having an enclosed cockpit. Deliveries of this fighter, already mentioned in connection with the Soviet I-153, and in the design of which lightness and manoeuvrability were emphasised, began in 1938. On 1 April of the following year (the 21st birthday of the Royal Air Force) the maiden test flight occurred of the first Mitsubishi A6M Zero, in which the qualities mentioned were present in extreme degree. That this was no birthday present for the RAF will later become apparent.

	Span	Length	Seats	Loaded weight	Maximum speed	Service ceiling	Armament
USA							
Curtiss PW-8	32′ 0″	22′ 6″	1	3,150 lb	165 mph	21,700 ft	1 r-c m-g+1 h m-g
Boeing P-12E	30′ 0″	20′ 3″	1	2,690 lb	189 mph	26,300 ft	1 r-c m-g+1 h m-g
Grumman F3F-3	32′ 0″	23′ 3″	1	4,403 lb	264 mph	33,200 ft	1 r-c m-g+1 h m-g

	Span	Length	Seats	Loaded weight	Maximum speed	Service ceiling	Armament
ITALY							
Fiat C.R.32	31′ 2″	24′ 5″	1	4,110 lb	233 mph	29,500 ft	2 h m-g
Fiat C.R.42	31′ 10″	27′ 1″	1	5,060 lb	267 mph	34,450 ft	1 h m-g+1 r-c m-g
Macchi C.200	34′ 8″	26′ 10″	1	5,715 lb	312 mph	29,200 ft	2 h m-g
USSR							
Polikarpov I-15	32′ 0″	20′ 7″	1	3,027 lb	223 mph	29,500 ft	2 or 4 r-c m-g
Polikarpov I-16	29′ 6″	19′ 11″	1	2,960 lb	282 mph	30,450 ft	4 r-c m-g
JAPAN							
Kawasaki Ki-10	33′ 0″	26′ 2″	1	4,000 lb	246 mph	32,800 ft	2 r-c m-g
Mitsubishi A5M	35′ 6″	25′ 7″	1	3,545 lb	265 mph	32,000 ft	2 r-c m-g

6

Into Battle Again

The Polish and Dutch fighters already mentioned briefly now enter the story again, by reason of events. On 1 September 1939, the German army struck across the Polish frontier, with tanks and aircraft giving heavy support. Poland's air-defence force consisted of squadrons of single-seat P.Z.L. fighters, mostly of the P.11c model. These were already out of date, deliveries having ceased some three years earlier. The P.11c, in fact, was directly descended from the P.1, which was first flown in September 1929 – ten years almost to the day before the German attack. The most remarkable feature of this fighter was the gull form of the high-set wing. True, this was a feature also of the Berliner-Joyce P-16, which flew within a few weeks of the P-1; but the description gull wing was especially deserved by the Polish fighter because the inner sections of the wing tapered down to the

fuselage not only in chord, or width from front to rear, but in depth also, giving a strikingly graceful and bird-like effect. It was this feature (intended, as already explained, to improve the pilot's view), together with other points of merit, which won for Poland considerable export orders for P.Z.L. fighters of several models.

The pilots of the dainty little Polish fighters fought ferociously against the Germans as they advanced both in the air and on the ground; but no amount of heroism could increase the firepower or improve the speed of the P.Z.Ls, and Poland fell. The war spread through Scandinavia and Europe; the great air battles over France and Britain were fought and won; then Italy invaded Greece. This nation had been among the purchasers of P.Z.Ls, and these, together with a handful of Bloch MB-151s, consti-

Seen in the red and white chequered markings of the Polish Air Force are P.Z.L. P.11c gull-winged fighters, of the type in which Polish pilots fought so valiantly in 1939.

tuted the defending air force. As in Poland, the P.Z.Ls were flown with telling effect; but although they could not win the day they showed what a fighter of good design could achieve, though the essentials of design were over ten years old.

If these Polish fighters were too old, then the Dutch Fokker G.I now associated with them was too new. There were curious links between this last of the great line of Fokker fighters and the Vickers *Destroyer* of 1913: both had created something of a sensation at

a public exhibition (the Fokker at the Paris Aero Show of 1936); both were named to impress their viewers (the Dutch machine was labelled in French *Le Faucheur – The Reaper*); and both were of twin-boom type, though the Fokker was of twin-engined tractor type whereas the *Destroyer* was a single-engined pusher. With its intended armament of nine machine-guns, or two cannon and three machine-guns, the Fokker G.I was second in firepower only to Germany's Me 110 and possibly the French Potez

631, which, at about the time the Netherlands was invaded, was having its armament increased. However, cannon expected from Denmark did not arrive, and some of the few available G.Is went into battle with only four machine-guns in the nose. The Netherlands was overrun in its turn, and the Battle of Dunkirk was only weeks ahead.

The fighter especially associated with Dunkirk is the Boulton Paul Defiant, for it was in this battle that the type was first in action. The circumstances recall the introduction of the Bristol Fighter in 1917.

Early claims by Defiant gunners for enemy aircraft destroyed appeared to confirm the idea of the turret fighter as a correct one; but this was to be quickly and grimly reversed. One reason for this was that the German pilots had at first mistaken the Defiants for Hurricanes and attacked from the rear as usual, only to expose themselves to the concentrated fire of four Browning guns. Learning from their mistakes, they attacked from below or ahead, and it was the heavy losses then sustained by the new British fighter (which had, in any case, inferior performance) that caused it to be withdrawn from front-line service. During 1941 the type was fitted with radar and served thereafter as a night fighter.

Although the Hawker Hurricane and Supermarine Spitfire had both seen action before Dunkirk it was in the ensuing Battle of Britain that these historic single-seaters fought side by side, with such effect that their names are as closely linked as those of David and Jonathan. This close association has sometimes obscured the considerable differences between them. In being low-wing monoplanes with a Rolls-Royce Merlin engine, retractable undercarriage and eight wing-mounted Browning guns they were identical; but the Spitfire was smaller, lighter, faster and had a slightly better rate of climb. Thus it was that the Hurricane was very widely employed to deal with the German bombers while the Spitfire engaged the Me 109 and Me 110 fighters. It is important to note, however, that both these British fighters were generally more manoeuvrable than their German opponents, especially in turning, though the Me 109 excelled in climbing and diving and had a higher service ceiling. Most of the German aircraft shot down were accounted for by Hurricanes, for these were used in greater numbers than Spitfires. For attacking the German bombers the Hurricane was superb, being a very steady gun platform, though increasing difficulty was encountered in penetrating the enemy's armour. Cannon would obviously be needed for future battles, but in the summer of 1940 only a few Spitfires carried this armament, whereas most of their opponents had two cannon in addition to two machine-guns. The German pilots were thus enabled to open fire at longer range.

The Hawker Hurricanes seen here were among the earliest to enter service with the RAF. They have adopted an 'echelon', or stepped, formation and the wheels of the middle one are being retracted.

The first British service-type fighter designed expressly for an armament of cannon, and the first twin-engined single-seat fighter to enter service with any air force, was the Westland Whirlwind. This

fighter was designed at a time when there was a marked growth of interest in the twin-engined arrangement, and it becomes necessary at this point to account for this interest. Here a little-known, but nevertheless historic, British experimental fighter, constructed as early as 1915, may be introduced. This was a twin-engined two-seat biplane built by Vickers and known as the F.B.8. One reason for using two engines in this aeroplane was to double the power available and so increase the speed. Another reason was that it enabled a gun to be installed in the nose without the use of synchronising gear, which at that time had not been developed in Britain. Somewhat similar considerations governed the design of the Whirlwind: the two Rolls-Royce Peregrine engines gave it a higher speed (at low altitude at least) than other fighters of the period, and the absence of an engine in the nose made it possible to group the very formidable armament of four 20-mm cannon very closely together, providing a very dense concentration of fire. Other considerations concerning twin-engined fighters will be touched upon in connection with the German Me 110. Meanwhile it must be recorded that the Whirlwind, because of various difficulties, and in view of its high performance at low levels, was converted into a fighter-bomber; and another historic British two-seat fighter now enters the story.

This aeroplane was not in itself remarkable, being nothing more than a stop-gap conversion of the Bristol Blenheim bomber, armed with five fixed machine-guns and a sixth gun in a turret. Nevertheless, the Blenheim IF, as it was known, was historic because it was the first type of fighter to go into action equipped with radar, enabling it to locate its target in darkness. Radar-equipped Blenheims were ready for service during the German bomber offensive against Britain during 1940–41, and though handicapped by a relatively poor performance scored their first victory on 22 July 1940.

Most of the kills by night during the 1940–41 offensive were made by another historic twin-engined Bristol type, and this yet another adaptation of a bomber, though far less handicapped on this account than the Blenheim IF. The new aircraft, the Beaufighter, was taken into service during July–September 1940, and its curious name is explained by the fact that many parts of its structure were identical with those of the Beaufort torpedo-bomber-reconnaissance aircraft. The main armament of four 20-mm cannon was located well back in the fuselage, leaving the nose free for the radar installation, and the cannon were quickly supplemented by six machine-guns in the wings. At first the cannon were fed from magazines containing sixty shells only, and the second crew-member had to act as loader, but later a continuous system of feeding was introduced.

Yet a third type of night fighter used by the RAF was another adapted bomber, in this instance of United States manufacture. Known as the Douglas Havoc, the type was armed with one free and eight fixed machine-guns and carried also the somewhat cumbersome radar of the period. Recalling some of the suggestions made before 1914 for bringing down airships, a number of Havocs were converted to operate with a device known as 'Pandora', this being the code-name for an explosive device trailed 2,000 ft below the Havoc in the path of enemy bombers. Other aircraft of the type were fitted with a Turbinlite of 2,700-million-candlepower, the batteries for which were stowed in the bomb compartment. These Turbinlite Havocs carried no armament but were fitted with special lights above the wing which enabled Hurricanes to fly in formation with them. It was planned that the Havoc, having located a bomber by radar, should provide illumination, enabling the Hurricanes to close in for the kill. Neither scheme succeeded.

As the great air battles developed so did the war at sea make increasing demands for specialised aircraft. It has already been noted that in the months preceding the war the Royal Navy had adopted as a successor to the Hawker Nimrod a version of the Gloster Gladiator known as the Sea Gladiator. Both these Gloster biplane fighters were in action, and the legendary *Faith*, *Hope* and *Charity*, defenders of Malta in 1940, were of the latter type. With the coming of the Hurricane and Spitfire, however, the Navy itself expressed a need for an eight-gun monoplane fighter, and this came into being in 1940 as the Fairey Fulmar, an adaptation of a light bomber. Whereas the Blackburn Skua, as previously mentioned, had all its guns concentrated in a turret, the pilot being unarmed, the Fulmar's guns were all controlled by the pilot, a second crew-member acting as navigator. Although a fine and welcome aeroplane the Fulmar inevitably suffered, like the Defiant, from a relatively low performance and inferior manoeuvrability, and sustained heavy losses accordingly. Fortunately for the Navy, the Hurricane, with suitable strengthening to enable it to be launched by catapult, became available to them, and in 1941 the Sea Hurricane came into service. Some of these aircraft were conversions of Hurricanes which had flown in the Battle of Britain; they were operated not from aircraft carriers but were catapulted from the decks of special merchant ships for use against the Focke-Wulf Fw 200 Condor reconnaissance-bombers then harrassing the Allied merchant ships. If out of range of land, which was usual, the Hurricat, as the fighter became known, had to come down in the sea, in the hope of the pilot being rescued by the ships he was protecting. Later,

Sea Hurricanes were operated from aircraft carriers.

At the outbreak of war the German first-line fighter squadrons were equipped with two types only, the Messerschmitt Me 109 and Me 110, and both of these are now described in the forms in which they were used in the Battle of Britain. The versions of the Me 109 concerned were of the E series, indicating that the type had already undergone considerable development. The Me 109E first appeared on the production lines in 1938 and the equipment of squadrons began in 1939. The engine was a Daimler-Benz DB 601 inverted-vee twelve-cylinder unit of 1,100 hp, nearly twice the power, that is, that had been available to the first Me 109s in service. The most usual armament was two synchronised rifle-calibre machine-guns mounted forward of the cockpit and two 20-mm cannon in the wings. The cannon were of Swiss Oerlikon type and lacked the hitting power of the French Hispano type. Nevertheless, as already mentioned, they gave the Me 109 an advantage over the Hurricane and Spitfire. The machine-guns had 1,000 rounds of ammunition (cartridges) each; the two cannon magazines each contained 60 rounds. Some Me 109Es had four machine-guns and no cannon. Numerous modifications, or alterations, were later made, including installation of 'Ha Ha'. This was the code-name for GM 1, a system whereby nitrous oxide, or laughing

General Vuillemin, in the uniform of the French Air Force, inspecting Messerschmitt Me 109Cs in company with German officers. These early Me 109s have the Junkers Jumo 210 engine.

gas, was injected into the supercharger to provide additional oxygen and increase the power of the engine.

The twin-engined two-seat Me 110 was first air-tested in the spring of 1936. It had been designed as a strategic, or long-range, fighter, capable of escort work or the destruction of enemy bombers, and it was known in Germany as a Zerstörer (destroyer), echoing the name of the 1913 Vickers biplane. The first production models (Me 110B) were too late for testing in realistic conditions in Spain, as the early Me 109s had been. It was recognised, however, that, although fast, having a speed approximating to the Hurricane's, the type must inevitably prove inferior to opposing single-seaters in manoeuvrability and possibly in rate of climb. Powered, like the Me 109E, with the excellent DB 601 engine, the type became the Me 110C, and it was this version that fought in the Battle of Britain. Armament was two 20-mm cannon and four rifle-calibre machine-guns, fixed and firing forward, and a free machine-gun at the rear; but as manoeuvrability was not always adequate in bringing the main fixed, or primary, armament to bear on the target, the type usually fared very badly in battle with the British eight-gun fighters.

About a year after the Battle of Britain had begun Germany invaded the USSR. Many of the defending squadrons were still equipped with I-15s and I-16s of various models and with I-153s; but although the last-named fighter, with its speed of nearly 270 mph, was the fastest biplane ever to enter service, and although the I-16 was even faster, the Russians had foreseen the need for monoplanes of much higher performance, and these were coming into use throughout 1941. All were of low-wing type with liquid-cooled engine and partly of wooden construction.

The most important of the new fighters, in numbers at least, was the LaGG-3, the curious combination of initial letters signifying that it had been designed by Lavochkin, assisted by Gorbunov and Gudkov. Comparatively small and light, the LaGG-3 achieved a good performance and was used with a variety of armament combinations, typical of these being a 20-mm cannon firing through the airscrew shaft, one heavy machine-gun and one rifle-calibre machine-gun. With five machine-guns, three of which were of heavy type, the LaGG-3 was used to escort the famous Ilyushin Stormovik armoured ground-attack aircraft.

The MiG-1 (Mikoyan and Gurevich) was a very fast fighter indeed, not only in having a speed of 390 mph but because the first example was designed and built in four months; but it was not a pleasant aeroplane to fly and was insufficiently manoeuvrable. It was quickly succeeded by the MiG-3. This type still lacked manoeuvrability, and though it had a very high performance at altitude, it was at first inadequately armed, with one heavy and two rifle-calibre machine-guns. Later two of the heavier guns were added.

The most successful of the new Soviet fighters was the fast yet manoeuvrable Yakovlev Yak-1. At the time of the German attack no fighters of this type were in front-line service, and as a safety precaution the production facilities were quickly moved some hundreds of miles to the east. Yet – such was the Soviet Union's war effort – the new fighters were coming off the production lines within a month of the move being completed. Although having a short range and relatively light armament (typically one cannon and one heavy machine-gun) the Yak-1 must be considered one of the more significant fighters, if only because it was the first of about 37,000 Yak fighters built during the war years.

During the course of the war the Russians made use of several types of American and British fighters, and first among these were the Bell Airacobra and Curtiss Tomahawk, the Tomahawk being a development of the Hawk monoplane mentioned earlier but having a liquid-cooled engine. The Airacobra, however, was strikingly unconventional in design. Its principal feature was a buried engine installation amidships, the tractor airscrew being driven through a ten-foot extension shaft. Not only did this arrangement allow a cannon to fire through the hollow shaft but it enabled the pilot to be placed well forward, where he had a better view than otherwise. Another remarkable feature for a single-engined fighter of the period, though it had been used a little earlier on the twin-engined Lockheed Lightning, was the nose-wheel, or tricycle, undercarriage. This type of undercarriage improves the pilot's view and makes landing easier, and is generally used on today's jet-propelled fighters. The Allison engine was not highly supercharged and the Airacobra had a relatively poor performance at height; but it was used very successfully by the Russians and Americans as a ground-attack aircraft, as was its successor the Kingcobra.

Some important types of American fighter under development at this time will be studied in Chapter 8.

	Span	Length	Seats	Loaded weight	Maximum speed	Service ceiling	Armament
POLAND							
P.Z.L.P.11c	35′ 2″	24′ 9″	1	3,960 lb	242 mph	36,000 ft	2 or 4 r-c m-g
NETHERLANDS							
Fokker G.I	56′ 3″	37′ 9″	2	10,560 lb	295 mph	30,500 ft	9 r-c m-g

	Span	Length	Seats	Loaded weight	Maximum speed	Service ceiling	Armament
GREAT BRITAIN							
Boulton Paul Defiant	39′ 4″	35′ 4″	2	8,318 lb	304 mph	30,350 ft	4 r-c m-g
Hawker Hurricane I	40′ 0″	31′ 11″	1	6,600 lb	324 mph	34,200 ft	8 r-c m-g
Supermarine Spitfire I	36′ 10″	29′ 11″	1	5,784 lb	365 mph	34,000 ft	8 r-c m-g
Bristol Beaufighter I	57′ 10″	41′ 4″	2	20,800 lb	323 mph	28,900 ft	4 c+6 r-c m-g
GERMANY							
Messerschmitt Me 109E	32′ 4″	28′ 4″	1	5,523 lb	354 mph	36,000 ft	2 c+2 r-c m-g
Messerschmitt Me 110C	53′ 5″	39′ 8″	2	15,300 lb	349 mph	32,000 ft	2 c+5 r-c m-g
USSR							
LaGG-3	32′ 2″	29′ 1″	1	6,316 lb	353 mph	33,450 ft	1 c+1 h m-g+1 r-c m-g
MiG-3	33′ 9″	26′ 9″	1	7,390 lb	397 mph	38,350 ft	1 h m-g+2 r-c m-g
USA							
Bell Airacobra	34′ 0″	30′ 2″	1	7,075 lb	368 mph	33,300 ft	1 c+2 h m-g+4 r-c m-g
Curtiss Tomahawk	37′ 3″	31′ 9″	1	7,325 lb	352 mph	32,400 ft	2 h m-g+2 r-c m-g

7

Global Combat: Japan, Germany

Between the Japanese attack on Pearl Harbor on 7 December 1941, and the final surrender of Japan on 14 August 1945, fighters were being developed at a rate and on a scale hitherto unknown. The most important factor in this massive advance was jet propulsion, but there were other well-kept secrets which had a dramatic effect on the course of the war. Prominent among these was the Japanese fighter which had first been flown on the RAF's 21st birthday in 1939.

Some of the problems confronting the designer of a naval deck-landing fighter have already been listed, and it might well be supposed that such a specialised machine would always be inferior to one less encumbered. Not so the famous Zero, or Mitsubishi A6M Reisen (Zeke), to give this Japanese fighter its full title, inclusive of Allied code-name.

(Such names became necessary as the Far East war developed not only for identification but because of the somewhat complicated Japanese system of naming and numbering their aeroplanes.) Pressed swiftly into service as the A6M2, the deadly new fighter was first in action over China in August 1940; yet warning of its existence had never reached the American pilots at Pearl Harbor. It is true that the Zero owed something of its excellent performance to the absence of self-sealing (after perforation by gunfire) petrol tanks and armour plate, which had, by this time, become normal protective equipment on fighters; but the rudest of shocks awaited those who had smugly supposed that Japanese aeroplanes were copies of Western types. Japan's new fighter dominated the Pacific until early 1943; but in spite of improvements the Allies gradually won superiority.

The later Mitsubishi J2M Raiden (Thunderbolt) was a specialised intercepter, or home-defence, fighter. It had several fine qualities but was plagued with troubles, though fighters of this type were used to defend Japan staunchly till the end.

The other great names in the construction of Japanese fighters were Kawasaki, Nakajima and Kawanishi. Toryu (Dragon Killer) was the name of the Kawasaki Ki-45 twin-engined two-seat counterpart of the German Me110. For attacking bombers at night many fighters of the type had two upward-firing heavy machine-guns or 20-mm cannon. Unusual among Japanese fighters in having a liquid-cooled engine, of the German DB 601 type, was the single-seat Kawasaki Ki-61 Hien (Swallow), another type extensively employed in defence of the Japanese homeland; and it was a shortage of these engines which led to one of the most remarkable Japanese fighters of all. The difficulty of installing an air-cooled radial engine in an airframe (aeroplane less engine) designed for an inline engine can readily be understood; yet that is what the Kawasaki designers achieved in the Ki-100, a fighter developed from the Ki-61. The Ki-100 gave an excellent account of itself as an intercepter, and is generally considered to have been the finest fighter ever used by the Japanese Army. Another fighter developed as an intercepter was the twin-engined Kawasaki Ki-102.

The full style and title of this fine Japanese fighter was 'Nakajima Ki-44-IIb Army Single-seat Fighter Model 2B'. It was named Shoki (Demon) and fought fiercely in the defence of Japan.

This had originally been intended for ground attack and was armed accordingly with a very large cannon of 57-mm calibre. While engaged on a test flight one of the earliest aircraft of the type encountered a formation of American Superfortress bombers, and with a single shot from its cannon destroyed a complete engine on one of the bombers.

From the Nakajima works came a series of fine radial-engined single-seaters. The very elegant Ki-43 Hayabusa (Peregrine Falcon) was in action over Malaya, Burma, Sumatra and Java, and rivalled the Zero in popularity among pilots. The Ki-44

Shoki (Demon) was an intercepter of somewhat similar design, but emphasising speed and climb at the expense of manoeuvrability; and similar again was the Ki-84 Hayate (Gale), which surpassed the opposing P-47 Thunderbolt and P-51 Mustang escort fighters in rate of climb and manoeuvrability. Growing shortages of light alloys, the metals generally used in the construction of fighters during the Second World War and also at the present day, led to experiments in the building of Hayates in wood. Greatly contrasting in design and purpose were the J1N1-S Gekko (Moonlight), a twin-engined night fighter, one version of which had not only two upward-firing cannon but two downward-firing cannon also, and the Nakajima A6M2-N seaplane. This last-named fighter was a conversion of the Mitsubishi Zero and was used in action against American bombers. Yet another remarkable Nakajima type was the C6N Saiun (Painted Cloud), a single-engined three-seat reconnaissance aircraft which was so fast that it could usually avoid interception. This was another type which was pressed into service as a night fighter, with upward-firing cannon.

The Kawanishi fighters included the N1K1 Kyofu (Mighty Wind), a seaplane built, like the Nakajima A6M2-N, to accompany amphibious landing forces in areas where there were no airfields. Like the A6M2-N also, this was in action against American bombers. Even more remarkable, for the reverse was usually true, it was developed into a landplane, this having two variations, the N1K1-J and N1K2-J Shiden (Violet Lightning). The second of these is generally considered to have been the finest Japanese naval fighter to enter service, and on one occasion a single fighter of the type is said to have destroyed four out of twelve Grumman Hellcats. The P1Y2-S Kyokko (Aurora) was yet another bomber converted for night fighting. One experimental version had no fewer than ten forward-firing cannon.

On 3 September 1943, nearly two years before the final defeat of Japan, the Italians surrendered, and before reviewing the fighters of the Powers remaining in the war brief reference may be made to the more notable Italian types. The finest of these were the Fiat G.55, which had an armament of three cannon and two heavy machine-guns, and the generally similar Macchi M.C.202 and 205. With its speed of 370 mph the M.C.202 showed a marked superiority over the Hurricane and other fighters in the Western Desert. Of a series of Reggiane fighters the 390-mph Re 2005 was the finest. It was estimated that with a Campini jet, which was not of the turbojet type later described but had a piston engine to drive the compressor, a speed of about 450 mph might be attained; but this was one of the war's many might-have-beens, and the true beginnings of the jet-propelled fighter are to be found in a maiden flight accomplished on 27 August 1939.

The aircraft concerned on that occasion, the German Heinkel He 178, was not itself a fighter; but it was the work of a company greatly skilled in the building of high-speed aircraft, and one which was soon to construct the first fighter in the world to have the new form of turbojet powerplant. This fighter was the He 280, which, although it did not go into production, was of high significance, not only in having the new kind of engine but in introducing also the ejection seat, a safety device to which hundreds of pilots now owe their lives. As the name suggests, this form of seat fires the occupant clear of the aircraft, a procedure which became necessary when speeds crept upward of 500 mph and as manoeuvring at such speeds produced in the pilot's body heavy loadings of g (force of gravity). In a turn, for example, he would be pressed down very hard in his seat.

The turbojet engine is one of a number of types of engine used to provide jet propulsion, sometimes called reaction propulsion because the engine, and the aeroplane of which it forms a part, reacts to the rearward squirting of a stream of hot gases by moving forward. The aeroplane moves, in other words, according to Newton's famous law of equal and opposite reaction. At the front of the engine is an open tube, or duct, into which air rushes. This air is compressed by a revolving compressor and is then delivered to one or more combustion chambers into which fuel (originally ordinary paraffin or kerosene) is injected. Here the mixture of fuel and air is ignited, heated and expanded. Being unable to escape forward, the hot gases rush backwards through a jet pipe, or nozzle, at the rear. On their way backwards they pass through a turbine, the purpose of which is to drive the compressor at the front.

Being capable of delivering a very high thrust (the equivalent of horsepower in a piston engine) the turbojet was an obvious choice for fighters; but before the later types of German jet fighter are reviewed some account must be given of the development of piston-engined fighters during and after 1942.

The Messerschmitt Me 109, first flown in 1935, continued in development throughout the war, and, indeed, until late 1956. The last of the line were built in Spain and were powered with British Rolls-Royce Merlin engines – a remarkable twist of fate for, as may be recalled, the first Me 109 of all was powered with a Rolls-Royce Kestrel. Aircraft of the much-improved Spanish type were used in making the film *The Battle of Britain*, and were among the last of some 35,000 Me 109s of various models. Thus, more examples of this great German fighter were built than of any other type, German or Allied.

After the Me 109E came the series F and G, these three most famous members of the family being known to German pilots as Emil, Friedrich and Gustav. The Me 109F was more powerful, had a finer fuselage shape and a wing of increased span, with rounded tips. Manoeuvrability was improved, as well as performance, and Friedrich was generally superior to the contemporary Spitfire V. As 1942 drew to a close Gustav began to come upon the scene, and this was a classic example of a fighter undergoing development almost to the limit, with even larger engine and heavier armament. Beauty of line now suffered as two heavy machine-guns were introduced in place of the earlier rifle-calibre guns, resulting in unsightly blisters. The heaviest armament generally carried was the two heavy machine-guns and three cannon. Some Gs had pressurised cockpits, and a water-methanol power-boosting system was also introduced on aircraft of this type. Both these features were introduced on other types of German and Allied fighters. A pressurised cockpit is one in which the internal pressure is maintained at a certain level whatever the pressure may be outside, and its purpose is to keep the pilot comfortable and efficient at high altitudes where the air is thin. Among the unpleasant effects of insufficient pressure at height is the formation of bubbles round the joints, resulting in a very painful experience known as the bends. The

water-methanol power-boosting system supplies a mixture of these two substances to the engine to provide additional oxygen and thus increase the power delivered. The effect is thus similar to that of the laughing gas system referred to in connection with the Me 109E.

For attacking bomber formations the Me 109G carried two massive 21-cm unguided rockets in tubes under the wing – another development foreshadowing the missile-armed fighter of today. The Me 109H was a long-span high-altitude development and the K model outwardly resembled the G. The K was the fastest of the series, attaining 452 mph.

Development of the less successful Me 110 was not spectacular, though the type was quite extensively used as a bomber and radar-equipped night fighter, carrying three, or even four, crew members.

The wartime achievements of Messerschmitt were vastly greater than those already described, impressive though these are; but the types immediately following, the Me 210 and 410, were not among the more successful. Mention of these twin-engined two-seaters may be confined to armament: the two rearward-firing heavy machine-guns were installed in remotely controlled barbettes, or small unmanned turrets, on the fuselage sides, and for attacking bombers as many as six fixed cannon and two heavy machine-guns were installed. Some Me 410s

Close-up of an Me 262, showing the installation of the turbojet engines under the wing, the ports in the nose for two of the four cannon and armour plate in the cockpit to protect the pilot's head.

had a 50-mm gun, projecting several feet ahead of the fuselage.

In many ways the most remarkable fighter of the war – one, indeed which can truly be described as revolutionary – was the single-seat twin-jet Me 262,

the first German jet fighter to enter service (late 1944). Its full employment as a fighter, however, was delayed by Allied bombing and by Hitler's insistence that many aircraft of the type be converted for use as bombers. Over 1,400 Me 262s were, in fact, completed, and many people believe that had these been used as fighters one year earlier the outcome of the war might well have been different. There were several fighter versions. The standard type in service had two Junkers Jumo 004 turbojets and four 30-mm cannon, of a new short-barrelled type, grouped neatly in the nose of the remarkable triangular-section fuselage. This shape enabled the maximum amount of fuel to be carried, for in this regard the new jets were heavy in their demands. There were many special developments, all more or less experimental, and these included night fighters. Some idea of how cleanness of external form was necessary to the very high speeds now being attained (the Me 262 was about 100 mph faster than piston-engined fighters then in service) is conveyed by the fact that the radar installation reduced the speed by nearly 40 mph. Also carried externally on some Me 262s in service were batteries of twenty-four small rocket missiles.

Notwithstanding the new standard of performance set by the Me 262 an even higher rate of climb was required for the interception of the massive bombing raids now threatening the continuance of Germany's war effort. One version was therefore built with a rocket unit that could be dropped after use; another had rockets built in with the turbojets. But although these mixed-power intercepters foreshadowed a class of fighter exemplified today by the French Dassault

Mirage III they never entered service. The first rocket-propelled fighter to achieve this distinction was, in fact, yet another Messerschmitt, the Me 163, and this had no other power unit than its Walter liquid-fuel rocket engine. Although an engine of this type uses fuel at a far higher rate even than a turbojet it has the advantage that its thrust does not decline at high altitudes, the reason being that it carries its own oxygen with it and does not depend on the outside atmosphere in any way. For the chemistry-minded, the fuel, or propellant, was T-stoff (hydrogen-peroxide and water), and the catalyst used with it was C-stoff (hydrazine hydrate and methyl alcohol). It may be added that although the Me 163 was the only wartime fighter in service having a rocket engine as its prime mover the Walter company also made rockets for assisting the take-off of heavily laden aircraft, and among these was the Me 262.

The rocket fuels were dangerous, both to the pilots and the crews who handled them on the ground, and there were many accidents; yet Me 163s achieved a number of successes against American bombers, partly by reason of their fantastic rate of climb (30,000 feet in 2·6 minutes), and their speed of nearly 600 mph. Endurance under power, after climb to altitude, was only $2\frac{1}{2}$ min, but this could be increased by periods of gliding. Two short-barrelled cannon were built in to the fuselage and provision was made

The Messerschmitt Me 163 was the first rocket-propelled fighter to go into service. The wheels shown here were dropped after take-off and the landing was made on the skid.

for either twenty-four unguided rocket projectiles under the wings or four such projectiles in each wing, firing vertically upward.

As already recorded, the Heinkel company built the world's first turbojet fighter, after having flown the first turbojet aeroplane of any kind. It has also been noted that the same company built one of the first fighters for the new German Air Force, and it may now be added that in 1935 the He 112 mono-

plane was built to compete with the Me 109. This it never succeeded in doing, though the type was built in small numbers and was used in the Spanish Civil War. The later He 100 was also built in small numbers, but the comparatively little known He 219 was ordered into production as a standard night fighter. This twin-engined monoplane had a nosewheel undercarriage and apart from being heavily armed was very fast, in some of its forms being able to destroy

British de Havilland Mosquitoes – supposedly almost free from interception by reason of their speed and height. Typically, the He 219 had a speed of 419 mph, had four or six cannon firing forward and two firing upward. It is claimed that one He 219 pilot destroyed five RAF bombers in one sortie.

Although the pioneer He 280 was never produced in numbers there was a second type of Heinkel turbo-jet fighter which was ordered in very large numbers indeed, the proposed output being one thousand a month. Designed, built and flown in the almost un-believable time of 69 days, this tiny monoplane, the He 162 Volksjäger, or People's Fighter, had a single BMW turbojet mounted on top of the fuselage, and represented another attempt to build a light, cheap *type jockey*.

Just over a hundred He 162s had been completed when Germany surrendered; and that this surrender was not brought about by failure on the part of Ger-many's fighter designers is now emphasised by reference to a type of single-seater which many experts believe possessed desirable fighting qualities in higher degree than any other – German or Allied. This was the Focke-Wulf Fw 190, first flown in June 1939, and first to surprise the RAF by its excellence about two years later. Among the most remarkable features was the BMW 801 air-cooled radial engine, with its cooling fan and carefully studied exhaust system. Although this engine was at first troublesome the Fw 190 soon proved to be much superior to the Spitfire V, and development continued throughout the war. Armament varied considerably according to period and purpose, one version having six cannon for attacking bombers.

For the Fw 190D a liquid-cooled inline engine was chosen, the radiator for which was mounted in the nose. This feature had not been common since the days of the Bristol Fighter, S.E.5a and SPAD; the Spitfire and Me 109, for example, had under-wing radiators and the Hurricane an installation below the pilot's cockpit. As the engine of the Fw 190D was longer than that originally used an extra section of fuselage was inserted behind the wings to compensate for it, and the result was not altogether pleasing to the eye. This fighter had an excellent performance, however, and in recognition of the ability displayed by the designer Kurt Tank (who was fond of flying his own aeroplanes) the next development was called Ta 152. Thus the name of Tank was placed among those of Willy Messerschmitt; Ernst Heinkel; R. J. Mitchell, who designed the Spitfire; and Sir Sydney Camm, responsible for most of the Hawker fighters, including the Fury and Hurricane.

It seems appropriate to add at this point that a modern fighter is so complicated that it is often impossible to say which member of a team did the

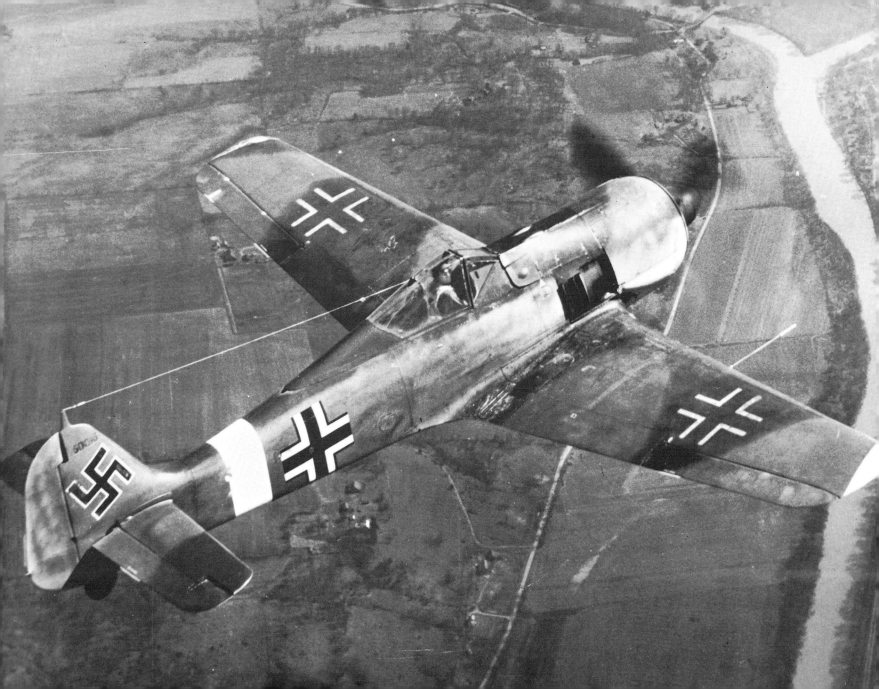

Like the antlers of a stag, radar aerials are seen projecting from this Ju 88C night fighter. The radar bore the code name 'Lichtenstein'. Guns were mounted in the nose and under the fuselage.

actual designing, this being the work of many minds and skills. In justice, too, it must be remarked that the designers of some of the earlier fighters have seldom been given the credit they deserve. Numbered high among these is Reinhold Platz, on whose drawing-board the finest Fokker fighters of 1914–18 took shape.

There were several versions of the Ta 152, and Tank also designed the Ta 154, a very fast night fighter designed to deal with the British Mosquito, and of wooden construction like its famous adversary. The Ta 154 was placed in production but never saw service in numbers: the contract was cancelled after

two aircraft of the type had crashed. It was found that the glue used in construction contained too much acid, causing the aircraft to come apart at the joints.

The most common German night fighters were in fact developments of the famous Junkers Ju 88 bomber, the first of which was the Ju 88C. This was regarded as an interim, or temporary, fighter and a more specialised development was the Ju 88G. The differences between this and the earlier models went considerably beyond the new vertical tail surfaces, of angular, instead of curved, shape. These differences concerned equipment, engines and armament. Apart from four or six forward-firing cannon and

◀ A remarkable study of a remarkable fighter. The pilot of this Fw 190 is turning his head to look up at the photographic aircraft. The installation of the BMW 801 engine was very neat.

various types of radar installation the Ju 88G some-times had two additional cannon firing upwards and forwards. An extremely formidable fighter was the Ju 388J with its four cannon forward and two heavy machine-guns in a turret located in the extreme tail. This turret was not occupied by a gunner, but was remote controlled from a forward position. Only three Ju 388Js were delivered, but about 6,000 Ju 88 fighters of various models had been made by the time of the German surrender.

Lesser used were conversions of Dornier Do 17 and Do 217 bombers. One early version of the Do 17 had its rear (free) gun so arranged that it could be fixed to fire forward and upward, and this led to several other installations of forward- and upward-firing guns, the most formidable being a group of four cannon on a Do 217. This kind of installation was known as Schräge Musik (Jazz); but for the Germans on 7 May 1945, the music was more solemn. Surrender was unconditional.

	Span	Length	Seats	Loaded weight	Maximum speed	Service ceiling	Armament
JAPAN							
Mitsubishi A6M	39′ 4″	29′ 9″	1	5,313 lb	332 mph	33,790 ft	2 c+2 r-c m-g
Nakajima Ki-84	36′ 10″	32′ 6″	1	7,965 lb	388 mph	34,450 ft	2 c+2 h m-g
ITALY							
Macchi M.C.205	34′ 9″	29′ 0″	1	7,515 lb	399 mph	36,090 ft	2 c+2 h m-g
GERMANY							
Messerschmitt Me 109F	32′ 6″	29′ 0″	1	6,055 lb	390 mph	37,000 ft	1 c+2 r-c m-g
Messerschmitt Me 262	41′ 0″	34′ 10″	1	14,100 lb	540 mph	37,565 ft	4 c+24 u-g m
Messerschmitt Me 163	30′ 7″	18′ 8″	1	9,500 lb	595 mph	39,500 ft	2 c+24 g m
Focke-Wulf Fw 190	34′ 5″	29′ 0″	1	9,750 lb	408 mph	37,400 ft	4 c+2 h m-g
Junkers Ju 88G	65′ 10″	54′ 1″	4	28,900 lb	363 mph	28,800 ft	6 c+1 h m-g

8

Global Combat: Great Britain, USA, USSR

Of all the Allied fighters which helped to bring about the defeat of Germany the British Supermarine Spitfire was the most famous, and throughout its long period of development retained much of its great beauty. Among the features contributing to its graceful appearance was what came to be known as the 'Spitfire wing', insect-like in form. This was, however, altered to meet special requirements: thus, for operation at extreme heights the wing span was increased, whereas for low-altitude work the beautiful pointed tips were entirely removed. In armament the first development after the eight machine-guns was two 20-mm cannon and four guns of the original type. Then followed four cannon, or two cannon and two heavy machine-guns. The Rolls-Royce Merlin engine was fitted with a two-speed two-stage supercharger, which meant that it could be made to rotate

faster at high altitude and that the fuel/air mixture was compressed by two successive impellers, one, in effect, supercharging the other. This type of supercharger enabled the Merlin to deliver considerably greater power at high altitudes, and this was one factor which enabled the Spitfire IX to fight the Focke-Wulf Fw190 on far more equal terms than the Spitfire V. So numerous were the variations in the basic design that the system of giving the mark number in Roman numerals became too clumsy, and after the Spitfire XX the numbers were given in Arabic figures. The larger Rolls-Royce Griffon engine, first introduced on the Mark XII, was fitted to all the final versions, the last of which was the Spitfire 24. Production finally ended in 1947. In ten years the engine power had more than doubled. Although weight had risen by 40 per cent the speed

No 19 Squadron, RAF, was the first to be equipped with Supermarine Spitfires, and proclaimed its identity as shown. The patchy camouflage was known as 'sand and spinach'.

had increased by 35 per cent and the rate of climb by 80 per cent. With folding wings and the inevitable

naval extras the Spitfire became the Seafire, and of both types a total of nearly 23,000 was produced.

Of the hardly less famous Hawker Hurricane little more remains to be said, for in the later stages of the war the type was used mainly as a bomber or for attacking tanks and other targets with heavy guns or rockets. Developments which must be mentioned, however, were the fitting of no fewer than twelve rifle-calibre machine-guns and the adoption of four cannon as the most common armament.

Although by reason of continual development the Spitfire remained an effective fighter throughout the war the Hurricane was incapable of being developed to anything approaching the same degree and was completely outclassed by two later Hawker fighters, the Typhoon and the Tempest. The most remarkable feature of the Typhoon, when it first appeared early in 1940, was the Napier Sabre 24-cylinder air-cooled engine of H cross-section. This engine gave the immense output of 2,100 hp, but proved at first unreliable, and this fact, together with badly de-signed features of the Typhoon itself, meant that the new fighter had a poor start in life. Performance at height was disappointing, but at low levels the Typhoon was the only fighter which could intercept with any certainty the Fw 190s engaged on sneak, or hit and run, bombing raids. As a ground-attack aircraft the type achieved its greatest fame.

One of the many troubles encountered by the Typhoon was buffeting (a sensation of being banged about) when diving at speeds around 500 mph. This prevented the pilot from aiming his cannon with accuracy. To overcome this and other difficulties the Tempest was given a wing of the new, thin, laminar-flow type. The term laminar flow meant that the thin layer of air next to the skin (the boundary layer) was prevented from becoming turbulent, or disturbed, and made to flow in layers, or laminations, thus decreasing drag.

Like the Typhoon, the Tempest was not one of the war's truly great fighters, but the people of Britain will not forget it as the destroyer of 638 of the 1,771 flying bombs brought down by the RAF.

The Bristol Beaufighter was succeeded as a night fighter by de Havilland Mosquitoes of various marks. The Mosquito was the second most versatile aircraft of the war (the most versatile of all being the Junkers Ju 88), and although it was originally built as an unarmed bomber the makers made provision at an early stage for offensive armament. It remained only to strengthen the wings, provide for radar and fit a bullet-proof windscreen to bring into being a night fighter which was to share the fame of its Bristol predecessor. Four cannon were fitted in the bottom of the fuselage, much as on the Beaufighter; but whereas the Beaufighter carried its six machine-guns

strung out along the wings the Mosquito had four such guns closely grouped in the nose. The speed was somewhat reduced by the radar and by the application of the matt, or non-shiny, black finish which had now become general for fighters of this class. This finish alone reduced the speed by 16 mph and was later abandoned. Performance was progressively increased by the installation of more powerful Rolls-Royce Merlin engines, and the original projecting arrow-head aerials for the radar gave place to a smooth nose with the adoption of a new type of radar with a spinning dish scanner, a rotating dish-like device for locating the target. The Mosquito was also used as a fighter-bomber, and aircraft of this type were used to escort some of the massive raids by RAF Bomber Command. Later these aircraft were replaced by specialised Mosquito night fighters.

The most highly specialised British fighter to be built in numbers during the war was the Westland Welkin. Unlike its predecessor the Whirlwind, this never entered service. Unlike the Whirlwind also it excelled at high, rather than low, altitudes, having been designed exclusively for the attack of high-flying bombers and reconnaissance aircraft. A twin-engined type somewhat resembling the Whirlwind, the Welkin was distinguished by its great wing span – no less than 70 ft – this being one feature associated with its high-flying capability. Another was the pilot's cabin, in which the air pressure at a height of 45,000 ft was equivalent to that experienced at 24,000 ft. This cabin was a self-contained unit made of bullet-resisting light metal, with an armour-plate bulkhead, or partition, at the rear.

Two British fighters of the Second World War remain to be mentioned, greatly contrasting in type and purpose. The first is the piston-engined Fairey Firefly deck-landing two-seater, cannon-armed, but following the general pattern of the Fulmar, and similarly handicapped. The second is the RAF's first jet-propelled fighter, the Gloster Meteor.

Work on jet propulsion was going ahead in England more or less on a parallel with that in Germany. In neither country was it known what the other side was attempting, and the most interesting fact which eventually emerged was that, whereas the Germans had chosen the long, slender axial-flow type of compressor, which thrust the air directly rearwards, the first of the British units were of the relatively short and plump centrifugal-flow variety, in which the air was first thrust outwards. In general layout the Meteor resembled the Me 262, having a turbojet unit on each wing; but the German fighter, although only slightly later in service, was more advanced in design and was over 100 mph faster than the Meteor I and nearly 50 mph faster than the Meteor III. Nevertheless the British fighter quickly

proved its worth; as early as 4 August 1944, a Meteor I destroyed a V 1 flying bomb by capsising it with a wingtip, the four cannon having refused to fire. On the same day a similar aircraft destroyed a V 1 with its cannon.

The technique of upsetting a flying bomb by disturbing the airflow round its wing was used by other British fighters and recalls instructions issued to British pilots during 1914. They were told that, on meeting a hostile aircraft, they should attempt to dive ahead of it and make a turn. One pilot recalled: 'The air pockets caused by this turn, I was assured, would be quite sufficient to send him crashing to the ground.' Air pockets would today be called turbulence.

The de Havilland Vampire, a second type of British jet-propelled fighter constructed in the Second World War, but which never saw service in that conflict, will be referred to in the next chapter; but among the fighters which did see action against the German V 1 jet-propelled flying bombs was the North American Mustang, and this outstandingly successful piston-engined fighter is accorded pride of place among the American types now to be considered.

In the sense that it was first built to a British order, that its design was influenced by British battle experience, and that it achieved its highest pitch of

The P-51B version of the North American Mustang, as shown, began to operate with the US Eighth Air Force in December 1943. Its long range enabled it to escort the American bomber formations.

development with a Rolls-Royce Merlin engine, the Mustang may be regarded as Anglo-American. The first Mustangs had the American Allison engine, which gave a relatively poor performance at height, and most of those supplied to Britain were used for low-level army co-operation duties. Late in 1942 the North American company redesigned the aircraft to take advantage of the two-stage two-speed Merlin which, fitted experimentally by Rolls-Royce, showed that an exceptionally high performance was attain-

able at the higher levels. Clearly, the Merlin and the Mustang were made for each other.

From December 1943 onwards Mustangs were escorting the bombers of the US Eighth Air Force. The astonishing success achieved in this rôle was partly due to the extremely efficient design (the Mustang had, among other advanced features, a laminar-flow wing), and partly also to the fitting of large drop tanks to increase the petrol supply, and consequently the range. These tanks could be

jettisoned when the fuel in them was consumed, thus freeing the Mustang of their drag and weight. Typical armament was six heavy machine-guns, and this was retained on the P-51H, the final, and fastest, version to enter service. Although this version was too late for operations over Europe it was in action in the final stages of the war against Japan. With its speed of 487 mph it was probably the fastest piston-engined fighter of the war. A development which did not see service until after the war was the astonishing Twin Mustang. This was, in effect, two Mustangs joined together, which meant that there were two pilots, one to relieve the other on the very long flights intended for the escort of Superfortress bombers. There were also two engines for reliability.

The two fighters with which the Mustang shared the honour and glory of escorting the great American bomber formations were the Lockheed Lightning and Republic Thunderbolt, and these contrasted greatly in design. The Lightning was of twin-boom layout, but unlike the old twin-boom pushers of 1914–18 was twin-engined also. The two engines were popular among pilots on long escort flights but somewhat impaired manoeuvrability in fighter-ver-sus-fighter actions. A device fitted on the later models to improve manoeuvrability was the manoeuvring flap, a flap which could be lowered in combat to increase the lift of the wing and decrease the risk of stalling, or falling because of lack of lift. A Lightning made American history in August 1942 when it became the first USAAF fighter to destroy a German aircraft – an Fw 200 Condor over the North Atlantic. With two drop tanks the P-38F model had a range of no less than 1,750 miles, the engines being throttled back to give a cruising speed of 213 mph.

The Republic P-47 Thunderbolt had a character all its own. It was the largest and heaviest single-seat piston-engined fighter ever built – and looked exactly that, with its enormously deep fuselage behind the massive eighteen-cylinder Pratt & Whit-ney air-cooled radial engine. In the last production-type Thunderbolts this engine delivered no less than 2,800 hp and was thus the most powerful piston engine to be used in a Service-type fighter during the Second World War. Six or eight heavy machine-guns was the standard armament and this was employed to excellent effect against aircraft on the ground as well as in the air. Thunderbolt pilots claimed, in fact, to have destroyed nearly as many aircraft on airfields as in combat, the respective figures being 3,315 and 3,752.

Another massive radial-engined American fighter was the US Navy's Vought Corsair, generally admitted to be the finest carrier-borne fighter of the war. Curious circumstances were associated with its introduction into service, for the US Navy at first

◄ Recessed into the tail booms of this Lockheed P-38 Lightning, in line with the rear portion of the wing, are the turbo-superchargers for the Allison engines. Note the grouping of the guns in the nose.

Massive, sleek, powerful, the Republic P-47 Thunderbolt was armed with six heavy machine-guns, disposed in the wings as seen. The cockpit enclosure is of 'clear view' type.

from land bases, 54,470; number flown from carriers, 9,581. Enemy aircraft destroyed in combat, 2,140; number of Corsairs lost in combat, 189. The original Corsair, flown in 1940, was the first American fighter to exceed 400 mph, and its most distinctive design feature was the inverted-gull wing. This means that the inner sections sloped downward from the fuselage.

The Grumman Wildcat has previously been mentioned as the first Grumman monoplane, and this same aircraft was operated by Britain's Fleet Air Arm as the Martlet. In order to increase the Wildcat's range the Americans experimented with towing fighters of this type behind other aircraft, with the Wildcat's engine stopped and the airscrew feathered, that is, with its blades turned edge-on to lessen resistance. The later Hellcat resembled a big Wildcat, and together with the Corsair helped to gain the advantage over the Japanese. Like the Corsair also, it was used as a night fighter, the radar equipment being carried in a pod, or streamlined container, under the wing. The Hellcat was by no means the end of Grumman's famous feline family, as the coming chapter will show. The next member was, in fact, the first twin-engined fighter to be put into production for service aboard aircraft carriers; but the fighter now to be mentioned also had a distinction of its own – being four-engined and having a wing

considered the type unsuitable for operation from carriers by reason of the pilot's poor view for landing and the high landing speed. Britain's Fleet Air Arm thought otherwise, and Corsairs supplied to that Service were in service aboard carriers about nine months before the US Navy was operating its own as intended. Two interesting sets of figures can be quoted in respect of the American Corsairs. Total sorties, or missions, flown, 64,051; number flown span of over 100 ft. As might be supposed, this was another conversion of a bomber – the Boeing Flying Fortress, in fact – and it was intended to act as an escort for bombers of the same type. Known as the B-40, it was armed with up to thirty heavy machine-guns and cannon. Twenty of the type were built for service, but the experiment was unsuccessful.

The largest and heaviest fighter in general service with United States squadrons was the Northrop P-61 Black Widow. Twin-engined, and having its tail carried on twin booms, this specialised night fighter had a fixed armament of four 20-mm cannon and a remote-controlled turret housing four heavy machine-guns. This turret could be locked so that the guns could be fired, together with the cannon, as fixed, forward-firing weapons. After a number of Black Widows had been built the turret was removed because it was found to cause buffeting, but it was later restored when a cure for the trouble was found.

Although the turbojet engine was pioneered in Germany and Great Britain, the USA managed to fly no fewer than four types of jet-propelled fighter during the war years – a fact that is often overlooked. It is true that none of these saw front-line service until after the war, and more will be said later concerning them; but for the sake of historical continuity the following must be placed on record. On 1 October 1942, only a year after work had begun, America's first jet fighter, the Bell XP-59A Airacomet, made its first brief hops. (An X before the type number of an American aeroplane denotes experimental.) The Airacomet had two General Electric turbojets, of British Whittle centrifugal-flow type, mounted at the junctions of the wings with the fuselage. On 8 January 1944, the first Lockheed XP-80 Shooting Star was flown. This was later built in large numbers and saw service in the Korean War, as will be described in the coming chapter. A single engine of Whittle type was fitted. On 25 June 1944 the first flight of the US Navy's Ryan XFR-1 Fireball took place. This was a mixed-power fighter, having one Wright Cyclone radial air-cooled piston engine and one Whittle-type turbojet in the fuselage behind the cockpit. (For the sake of scrupulous historical accuracy, the jet engine was not actually installed until the following month.) This hybrid type was able to fly on the power of the piston engine only, thus extending its range, the turbojet being kept in reserve for take-off, climb and maximum speed. Lastly, on 26 January 1945, the McDonnell XFH-1 Phantom was first flown for the US Navy. This fighter has a place in the following chapter as the forerunner of today's mighty Phantom II, which is, it is hardly necessary to add, a totally different aircraft.

The use by the Russians of the Airacobra, King-cobra and Tomahawk has already been mentioned,

Russian fighters were expected to operate in conditions of extreme cold, and this Lavochkin La-5
was appropriately photographed casting its shadow over the snow.

and to these types may now be added a development
of the Tomahawk known as the Warhawk. All these
American fighters were regarded mainly as ground-
attack aircraft, and for air combat the Russians produced some very fine fighters of their own. Two of
these, the La-5 and La-7, were radial-engined
developments of the LaGG-3 already mentioned.
Their sleek, compact appearance suggested what
they proved to be in combat: they were very fast, but

also possessed outstanding powers of manoeuvre. One
version of the La-5 was called La-5FN, the added
letters signifying Forsirovannii Nyeposredstvenny, or
boosted engine; but greatly more significant was a
development of the La-7 having a liquid-fuel rocket
in the rear fuselage. Fumes from the rocket fuel,
however, are said to have weakened the fuselage,
and mixed-power La-7s do not appear to have gone
into general service, though ordinary fighters of this

type were used by many of Russia's most successful fighter pilots.

From the Yak-1 previously mentioned was developed the Yak-3, and from the slightly larger Yak-7 the Yak-9 was derived. The last-named was used, between 1942 and the war's end, in greater numbers than any other Soviet fighter, and was flown by Polish and French units, as well as by Russian squadrons, to excellent effect. In combat with Me 109Gs the Yak-9 pilots tried to engage the German fighters at levels below 13,000 ft, where their performance was superior. Although small in size — much smaller even than a Mustang — the Yak-9 was developed as a long-range escort fighter, enabling it to accompany Soviet and Allied bombers.

The war was then nearing its end.

	Span	Length	Seats	Loaded weight	Maximum speed	Service ceiling	Armament
GREAT BRITAIN							
Supermarine Spitfire XVIII	36′ 10″	33′ 4″	1	9,320 lb	442 mph	41,000 ft	2 c+2 h m-g
Hawker Typhoon	41′ 7″	31′ 10″	1	11,400 lb	405 mph	34,000 ft	4 c
de Havilland Mosquito XI	54′ 2″	40′ 11″	2	20,000 lb	370 mph	34,500 ft	4 c+4 r-c m-g
Gloster Meteor III	43′ 0″	41′ 3″	1	13,300 lb	493 mph	44,000 ft	4 c
USA							
North American P-51D Mustang	37′ 0″	32′ 3″	1	11,600 lb	437 mph	41,900 ft	6 h m-g
Lockheed P-38J Lightning	52′ 0″	37′ 10″	1	21,600 lb	414 mph	44,000 ft	1 c+4 h m-g
Republic P-47D Thunderbolt	40′ 9″	36′ 1″	1	19,400 lb	428 mph	42,000 ft	6 h m-g
Vought F4U-1 Corsair	41′ 0″	33′ 4″	1	14,000 lb	417 mph	36,900 ft	6 h m-g
Grumman F6F-3 Hellcat	42′ 10″	33′ 7″	1	15,487 lb	375 mph	37,300 ft	6 h m-g
Northrop P-61A Black Widow	66′ 0″	48′ 11″	2	32,400 lb	369 mph	33,100 ft	4 c (+4 h m-g)
Ryan FR-1 Fireball	40′ 0″	32′ 4″	1	10,595 lb	426 mph	43,100 ft	4 h m-g
USSR							
Lavochkin La-7	32′ 2″	27′ 11″	1	7,495 lb	422 mph	34,450 ft	3 c
Yak-9U	32′ 10″	28′ 6″	1	6,985 lb	415 mph	34,000 ft	1 c+2 h m-g

9

Jets Supreme: USSR, Great Britain

When Germany surrendered in 1945 a wonderfully rich assortment of technical information, devices and weapons became available to the victorious Allies. The Russians were quick to take advantage of the idea of using sweptback wings, with the object of permitting higher speed, and this idea they wisely used in conjunction with a very fine British Rolls-Royce turbojet, made available to them by the United Kingdom Government. The result came as a great shock, as had the Mitsubishi Zero and Focke-Wulf Fw 190 of earlier years. This shock was especially great because a new class of air fighting had now been introduced: that is, combat between jet-propelled aeroplanes flying at speeds of about 600 mph.

It was unpleasant for the Americans, fighting in the 1950s a new air war in Korea, to find that a Soviet fighter completely outclassed the straight-winged Lockheed F-80 Shooting Star. It was even more unpleasant when they found that this same enemy fighter was in certain ways superior to the later North American F-86 Sabre, which itself had sweptback wings. One advantage the Sabre did possess was in having radar ranging for its guns. This device was the most notable advance in air gunnery after the British gyro gunsight, introduced into the RAF towards the end of the Second World War with the object of relieving the pilot of the task of making the very large allowances for speed and rate of turn necessary in high-speed combat. Another factor in the Sabre's favour was the American pilots' superior combat experience, for they were fighting Chinese pilots with relatively inferior training.

This record of historic events can now be followed by a review of Soviet fighters, and first by some remarks on the MiG-15, as the new Soviet fighter which appeared over Korea was known. This fighter was a very compact monoplane, with the wing set at the mid position. It was armed with one 37-mm cannon and two of 23 mm, installed in what would be called today a gun pack, this being a kind of self-contained mounting which allows the guns to be lowered from the fuselage for easy servicing. An ejection seat for the pilot's use in emergency was not at first installed, but was added later. Some of the MiG-15s had water injection for increasing the engine thrust for brief periods, and on some examples of the later MiG-17 a similar effect was obtained by the use of an afterburner, allowing extra fuel to be burned in the jet tailpipe. This is a common fitting on modern fighters.

Both the MiG-15 and MiG-17 had a single turbojet, but the earliest of the MiG jet fighters, the MiG-9 of 1946, had two turbojets. These were mounted not under the wings, as on the German Me 262 and British Gloster Meteor, but in the bottom of the fuselage.

The year 1953 saw the first flight of the MiG-19. This type had two turbojets in the fuselage and was the first Soviet fighter in service to be capable of flying faster than the speed of sound (that is, of exceeding Mach 1) in level flight. The speed of sound is about 760 mph at sea level and about 660 mph in the stratosphere. The stratosphere is the layer of the earth's atmosphere which extends above the troposphere, or the layer of the atmosphere in which we live. The upper limit of the stratosphere is about 31 miles. As the speed of sound varies, a Mach number is used to measure the speed of an aircraft in relationship to it; thus the speed of sound itself is Mach 1, half the speed of sound Mach 0·5, twice the speed of sound Mach 2. The term commemorates the name of the Austrian physicist Ernst Mach.

Mach 1 was first exceeded in level flight by the highly experimental American Bell X-1 on 11 October 1947; so by getting the MiG-19 into service by 1955 the Russians did well. It will later be seen, however, that in this respect they did rather less well than the Americans.

For their next fighter, the MiG-21, the MiG designers adopted a wing of delta (triangular) form, as originally developed in Germany. This form of wing is very favourable to the attainment of high speed, but although the MiG-21 achieves over 1,500 mph, this figure is about 300 mph below the corresponding figure for the MiG-23, described in the coming chapter.

The Lavochkin fighters previously mentioned were followed by others, some with piston engines and some with turbojets, but development of this fighter family has now come to an end. Whether the

The USSR's delta-wing MiG-21 has been supplied to the air forces of many allies and friends. Excellent fighter though it is, it is completely outclassed by the MiG-23.

same is true of the Yaks is not known. The last of the line on record is the Yak-28, a twin-jet two-seater of very striking appearance, partly by reason of two large guided missiles carried under the wing, together with the two massive turbojet power units. The Yak-28 is a development of the Yak-25, which was the Soviet Union's first twin-jet all-weather fighter.

The guided missiles just mentioned are known by the NATO code-name Anab, and two such missiles are also carried by the Sukhoi Su-9 single-seat single-engined delta-wing all-weather fighter, earlier versions of which carried four of the smaller Alkali missiles. An even more advanced Sukhoi delta-wing all-weather fighter is already in service. This is likewise a single-seater but has twin jets, and may be known as the Su-11.

The all-weather class of fighter, which now comes into the story for the first time, was developed from what was formerly called the night fighter, a class which, as already shown, was in service against German airships as early as 1916. As the Second World War advanced, however, it became clear that, to achieve the most certain possible kill in bad weather or at night, the fighter must be provided with every available aid. This became especially clear when very fast bombers of the Mosquito type began to be used, for these were over defended territory for a relatively short time. Radar, of constantly improved type, was an obvious aid; but radar had been used on the Blenheim fighter in 1940. Clearly, what was really needed was a weapon which would find its own way to, or home on, its target – a development of the unguided rockets which had earlier been used by Soviet and German fighters. Such a weapon would in any case become desirable for fighting in clear daylight because of the great speeds at which combats would take place, making it increasingly difficult for a pilot to bring his guns or unguided rockets to bear. Thus the Germans, already with considerable experience of rocketry, developed towards the end of the war the first air-to-air guided missile, called the X-4. The war ended before this could be used in action; but a deadly new weapon was now becoming available to the fighter.

Study of the fighter's own development is now resumed by reference to British types.

There will always be argument concerning the best piston-engined fighter built before jet propulsion changed the entire fighter scene by making possible entirely new standards of performance. There will always be arguments, too, as to what was the most beautiful fighter ever built. Very strong claims could be made on both accounts for the de Havilland Hornet, a twin-engined single-seater which, when first flown in 1944, reached the astonishing speed of 485 mph. True, this was reduced somewhat with the addition of equipment; but the Hornet, which entered service after the war both in single-seat and two-seat forms, was the realisation of many dreams.

The present chapter is headed 'Jets Supreme', and

de Havilland's first jet fighter was almost as different from the graceful Hornet as it could possibly have been. Indeed, so strange did it appear, with its tail carried on two booms, and its squat appearance generally, that, when it was first flown in September 1943, it was called the Spider Crab. Equally fitting was the official name Vampire, with which it was to become world-famous after the war when, for example, in July 1948, it became the first jet aircraft to fly the Atlantic. The later Venom was of similar appearance – and just as well-named. The twin-boom arrangement was retained for the massive twin-jet Sea Vixen all-weather deck-landing fighter which succeeded the Sea Venom in naval service.

The Vampire was Britain's second jet fighter, the first, as already noted, having been the Gloster Meteor. It has also been noted that the Meteor was an inferior aircraft to the wartime Me 262 and that the post-war MiG-15 took the whole world by surprise when it appeared over Korea. It can well be imagined, then, how Meteor pilots felt having first encountered MiGs in that war. The present writer recalls occasions when, after the pilots had returned from action, he would join them in a mournful little song beginning: 'All I want for Christmas is my wings swept back.' On the other hand he recalls an American pilot, on attachment to the RAF, declaring that the Meteor climbed 'like a home-sick angel'.

This was due to its good thrust/weight ratio, meaning that the two Rolls-Royce Derwent turbojets gave high thrust but that the Meteor itself weighed relatively little.

The Meteor was further developed for the RAF as a two-seat night fighter, the term all-weather being reserved for the next Gloster fighter, the Javelin. This was a massive delta-wing two-seater, and, though not altogether successful, served to introduce missiles into the RAF. Also, it was the first twin-jet delta-wing aircraft to fly. The English Electric Lightning, which replaced it, will be considered in a later chapter.

One of the greatest names in fighter history is that of Hawker, and this was kept in being after the war by the piston-engined Fury and Sea Fury, which somewhat resembled the Focke-Wulf Fw 190; the dainty jet-propelled Sea Hawk; and the handsome sweptwing Hunter. Like several other Hawker fighters, the Hunter was bought by many nations. Four 30-mm cannon formed the armament and the Hunter could dive at supersonic speed.

Even today the Hawker line is continued by the Harrier, though this is best considered as a strike aircraft rather than as a specialised fighter. It would be pleasing to record that the Spitfire also has a modern successor, or that the last of the Supermarine fighters were altogether worthy of one of the greatest names in fighter history. The facts are otherwise. In 1946 Supermarine flew their first jet fighter, which was later named Attacker. The most unusual feature was the tail-down undercarriage, a relic of the piston-engined Spiteful and Seafang from which the Attacker was developed. Far more modern in appearance was the Swift, the first British sweptwing fighter to enter service; but the Swift encountered severe difficulties and must be considered a failure. Last came the massive twin-jet Scimitar which, though it served the Royal Navy well from 1958 to 1965, can hardly be considered among the truly historic fighters.

The Scimitar was certainly among the largest and heaviest fighters of its day, but by the 1950s fighters in general were becoming greatly more complicated. This same period, however, saw one determined, if unsuccessful, attempt to revive the idea of the cheap, light fighter – the *type jockey* as earlier developed by the French. This attempt was made by the Folland company in Great Britain, the aircraft concerned being a tiny high-wing monoplane called the Gnat. Although extremely agile this little fighter lacked the ability to carry the increasing amount of equipment then coming into demand and found acceptance as a fighter only in India and Finland. The Gnats in RAF service are two-seat trainers. In order to save weight and complication the undercarriage of the Gnat was designed to serve also as an air brake. Air brakes are normally separate surfaces which can be extended to create air resistance and slow the aircraft in flight.

The light fighter idea was now finally dead, though a compromise, or middle-of-the-road type of fighter, the Northrop F-5, later achieved success and is referred to in the following chapter.

	Span	Length	Seats	Loaded weight	Maximum speed	Service ceiling	Armament
USSR							
MiG-15	33′ 1″	36′ 3″	1	11,270 lb	665 mph	51,000 ft	3 c
MiG-19	32′ 0″	37′ 6″	1	19,850 lb	860 mph	55,000 ft	2 c+8 u-g m
MiG-21	25′ 0″	55′ 0″	1	18,800 lb	1,320 mph	60,000 ft	2 c+2 or 3 g m
GREAT BRITAIN							
de Havilland Hornet	45′ 0″	36′ 8″	1	17,700 lb	472 mph	35,000 ft	4 c
de Havilland Vampire I	40′ 0″	30′ 9″	1	8,578 lb	540 mph	28,500 ft	4 c
Gloster Meteor F.8	37′ 2″	44′ 7″	1	19,100 lb	590 mph	44,000 ft	4 c
Hawker Hunter F.6	33′ 8″	45′ 10″	1	24,000 lb	715 mph	55,000 ft	4 c

10

Jets Supreme: USA, Sweden, France, Canada

As already recorded, America's first jet-propelled fighter, the Bell XP-59 Airacomet, was built in 1942. The type was ordered in some numbers as the P-59A and B, but proved unsatisfactory for its intended purpose. The name of Bell was then removed from the roll of fighter-builders. Names which did remain with prominence were those of Grumman, Lockheed, North American, Northrop, Republic and Vought, and to these were to be added Convair, Douglas and McDonnell.

No fewer than five of Grumman's famous cat family were to follow the Hellcat into service. The first of these, the F7F Tigercat, was the first twin-engined carrier-borne fighter to go into operation and the first US Navy fighter to have a nosewheel under-carriage. A piston-engined single-seater, the Tigercat carried the very formidable armament of four 20-mm cannon and four heavy machine-guns. A two-seat night fighter version was developed. The F8F Bearcat was generally of Hellcat type, but very much superior, and was the last of the piston-engined Grumman fighters, the first of the jets being the F9F Panther, first flown in 1947. The Panther had a straight wing and was the first US Navy jet fighter to go into action (August 1950). Its successor, the F9F Cougar, had a swept wing, and the completely redesigned F11F Tiger of 1954 was the first naval fighter to be capable of exceeding the speed of sound in level flight. Armament was four cannon and two or four Sidewinder missiles, carried under the wings.

The Sidewinder is perhaps the most widely used of all air-to-air missiles and dates from 1953. Designed by the United States Ordnance Test Station, it is notable for its simplicity. The moving parts number fewer than two dozen and there are no more electronic components than in a domestic radio set. The system of guidance can be either of radar type or of the kind known as infra-red homing, whereby the missile senses and homes upon the heat emitted by the target. It is claimed that the Sidewinder was the first air-to-air guided missile to destroy an enemy aircraft in combat, the occasion being the Quemoy crisis of 1958 when Chinese Nationalist pilots destroyed a number of Communist aircraft with this weapon.

It will later be shown that the Tiger is unlikely to have been the last US Navy fighter to bear the famous name of Grumman.

Lockheed followed the piston-engined Lightning with the jet-propelled Shooting Star, already mentioned in connection with the Korean War. This, in turn, was developed into the F-94 Starfire two-seat all-weather fighter which had a remarkable armament installation. Surrounding the radome, or circular dome covering the radar scanner in the nose, was a ring of twenty-four 2·75-in Mighty Mouse unguided rockets, and a pod carrying twelve of these little rockets could be fixed to each wing.

Early in 1954 Lockheed flew the first of the astonishing F-104 Starfighters. Around this type much controversy has arisen because of the very high accident rate, in German service, at least: but the Starfighter must nevertheless be recognised as one of the most remarkable fighters of all time. Although little used in its country of origin this aeroplane has been manufactured in Belgium, Canada, Germany, the Netherlands, Italy and Japan, and as its dagger-like shape is likely to be familiar to many readers of this book the type is selected for description in some detail.

The most remarkable of all the Starfighter's features is the wing. This is extremely short in span (21 ft 11 in), has no sweepback, is of exceptional thinness, razor-sharp, and has an anhedral angle (downward slope) of 10 degrees. Because the wing is so small and the wing loading so high the landing speed is high also. Among the high-lift devices required to reduce this speed is a system for controlling the boundary layer, that is the very thin layer of air next to the skin. This system entails bleeding air from the compressor of the turbojet which propels the aircraft and ejecting it over the hinged flaps which form the wing trailing-edge, when these flaps are lowered for landing.

The fuselage has a very long pointed nose, and

The Lockheed F-104 Starfighter came as a new shape in the sky. The extremely small span and area of the wing (seen here with fuel tanks at the tips) accentuated the length of the pointed nose. A German example is shown.

attached to each side at the rear is an air brake. Far forward towards the nose is the pilot's cockpit, air-conditioned as well as pressurised. To allow the pilot to get in and out the transparent canopy is hinged along one side. The pilot's ejection seat originally ejected downwards, but the direction was later reversed.

The engine was designed by the American General Electric company and is known as the J79. An after-burner is fitted, and this is apparent from the large

diameter of the jet tailpipe, located under the T-type tail. Air for the turbojet is taken in through two intakes, one on each side of the fuselage just forward of the wing. So heavy are the demands of the turbojet, especially with the afterburner working, that about 750 gallons of fuel are carried in the fuselage. Additional fuel can be carried in four external tanks, two at the wingtips and two under the wings. Fuel can be taken aboard in flight by means of a refuelling probe, the pilot manoeuvring the aircraft so that this engages with a drogue, or sleeve-like device, trailing behind the tanker aircraft.

The Starfighter was the first fighter to be armed with the amazing Vulcan 20-mm 'revolver cannon', operating on the principle of the old Gatling gun; that is, having a rotating group of barrels. Two Sidewinder missiles can be carried under the fuselage, another two under the wings and two more at the wingtips. Many different loads are possible for attacking ground targets, but the F-104 is considered here solely as a fighter.

As for performance, the Starfighter has a maximum level speed of Mach 2·2 at a height of 36,000 ft, which is equivalent to 1,450 mph. At low altitude the rate of climb is no less than 50,000 ft a minute, but the stalling speed (the speed at which the wing loses lift and fails to sustain the machine in the air) is also high at 144 mph. Although the service ceiling is 58,000 ft a 'zoom altitude' of 90,000 ft is attainable; but as the term suggests, this cannot be sustained. A final figure of interest is the time to accelerate to twice the speed of sound, namely three minutes.

The foregoing particulars relate to the most commonly used Starfighter, the F-104G. As a specialised intercepter fighter for Italy Lockheed have developed the F-104S, which, having a new afterburner, permitting higher thrust, can attain a Mach number of 2·4. Armament of this version consists of Raytheon Sparrow missiles. The Sparrow was originally developed for the US Navy but is also used by the USAF, the RAF and the Royal Navy. This weapon is 12 ft long, achieves Mach 2·5 and has a range of over eight miles.

After the piston-engined Twin Mustang already mentioned the North American company produced a straight-winged jet-propelled single-seater known as the FJ-1 Fury. This was the forerunner of the F-86 Sabre and F-100 Super Sabre, the former of which has already been referred to in connection with the Korean War. Whatever its shortcomings in that war the Sabre must be numbered among the truly great fighters and was among the first aircraft to attain supersonic speed, though this could be achieved only by diving and not in level flight. Having prevented the MiG-15 from gaining air superiority over Korea, the Sabre was developed as an all-weather fighter, known as the F-86D or 'Sabre Dog'. A remarkable feature of this version was the retractable pack of twenty-four Mighty Mouse unguided rockets which was lowered from the underside of the fuselage before the rockets were fired. Late aircraft of this type were among the first fighters to have a drag chute, that is, a parachute which can be streamed on landing to present resistance to the air and thus supplement the braking power of the wheel brakes. A US Navy fighter related to the Sabre was the F-1 Fury.

It was remarked earlier that the Russians did well to get the MiG-19 into service by 1955, this being their first fighter to be capable of supersonic speed in level flight. It was added, however, that they did rather less well in this respect than the Americans, and it must now be recorded that the first level-supersonic fighter to enter service was the North American F-100 Super Sabre. The first of these fighters went to the squadrons late in 1953, and although a series of accidents followed, the single-jet single-seat Super Sabre established itself as a remarkable 'first' in the Century Series of American fighters.

The Grumman cat family was almost equalled in extent by the Republic fighters bearing names beginning with Thunder. Three types which followed the Thunderbolt must be mentioned here, although these were used primarily as ground-attack aircraft. These types were the P-84 Thunderjet, a straight-wing type of 1946; the sweptwing F-84F Thunder-streak development of 1950: and the F-105 Thunder-chief of 1955. The F-105 was the heaviest single-seater ever taken into service, weighing in one form over 50,000 lb. Its Vulcan 'revolver cannon' was supplied with over a thousand rounds of ammunition and these could be discharged in a single burst lasting fifteen seconds.

In this listing of Republic fighters it will be noticed how the Americans' system of calling their fighters pursuit aircraft, as indicated by the P in P-84, gave way to the term fighter, represented by the change to F for the Thunderstreak.

A further point of interest is the way in which the American manufacturers gave their fighters names, the cats and Thunders having already been instanced. The piston-engined Vought Corsair, which had distinguished itself in the Second World War, was followed by other Vought fighters having buccaneering associations, the first of which was the F6U Pirate, a straight-wing jet-propelled single-seater. This was quite conventional in design, but the same can certainly not be said of its successor the F7U Cutlass, first flown in 1948. In appearance the Cutlass was, in fact, perhaps the most remarkable fighter ever taken into service, having no tail, a blunt sweptback wing, twin vertical assemblies attached to the wing and a cockpit enclosure of most impressive dimensions. Like the MiG-15, Sabre and other types, this fighter was based largely on German researches. It had two turbojets and could be armed with four Sparrow missiles.

The name of Vought continues until this day in association with the LTV (Ling-Temco-Vought) F-8 Crusader, which, although more conventional in design than the Cutlass, is unique among fighters in having a variable-incidence wing. This means that the angle at which the wing is tilted to the line of

◄ Showing the sweep of their wings as they turn in formation these North American F-100 Super Sabres also display their afterburners and national markings. The F-100 was America's first supersonic fighter.

flight can be altered to ensure the best possible range between maximum and minimum speeds.

The names which now remain to be added to those of the long-established builders of American fighters are those of Convair, Douglas and McDonnell.

Convair were among the companies who decided to profit from German research, and accordingly they consulted with Dr Alexander Lippisch who had been responsible for developing the delta wing. First they constructed the XF-92A, a flying scale model of a proposed fighter which was never built. Then, starting afresh, they built the F-102 Delta Dagger; but this proved to be much slower than expected, entailing a major redesign. It was this redesign which introduced a feature which was to become common on high-speed aircraft, namely the waisted or pinched form of fuselage, popularly known as the Coke bottle form. An aircraft having such a fuselage is said to have been designed according to the area rule, meaning that the cross-sectional areas of the wing and fuselage are so proportioned as to give minimum drag at supersonic speed. The Delta Dagger entered service as a fast intercepter fighter in the arming of which guns were discarded entirely. The sole armament was six Hughes Falcon missiles, carried internally, and twenty-four unguided rockets. The later F-106 Delta Dart carried two Genie missiles and up to four Falcons.

Into the story of fighter development now enters the most devastating weapon ever invented for this class of aircraft, namely the nuclear-tipped missile, or one having a nuclear instead of a conventional explosive warhead.

The first nuclear-tipped missile designed to be launched from a fighter was the Genie, development of which was begun by the Douglas company in 1955. As already noted, missiles of this type formed part of the armament of the Delta Dart; they were also carried by the Northrop Scorpion and McDonnell Voodoo, later mentioned.

A Genie was first tested in flight on 19 July 1957, the launching aircraft on this occasion being a Northrop Scorpion. The launch took place at about 15,000 ft and the pilot turned the aircraft sharply to avoid the effects of the explosion. After the Genie had travelled three miles it was triggered-off by a signal from the ground. In service the missile is launched automatically and the nuclear explosion is caused by a special fire-control system on the aircraft. The nuclear warhead remains inert, or harmless, until it is armed a few seconds before firing.

The Genie has no guidance system, the reason being that it was intended for use not against an individual aircraft but against a formation, the extent of the nuclear explosion rendering precise accuracy unnecessary. This missile weighs over 800 lb, is over $9\frac{1}{2}$ ft long, and has a range of six miles.

The other type of missile mentioned in connection with the Delta Dagger and Delta Dart – the Hughes Falcon – is in reality a whole family of weapons, for there are Falcons of several different types, including the even deadlier Super Falcon. In its original form the Falcon was the first air-to-air guided missile to be taken into service by the USAF. Falcons are 6–7 ft long, and a version with a nuclear warhead, called Nuclear Falcon, was the first guided missile of this class to enter service. The fighter concerned was the Delta Dagger.

The Northrop F-89 Scorpion, named as the test-aircraft for the firing of the first Genie, was the second of two large Northrop fighters used by the USAF, the first having been the Black Widow already mentioned. The Scorpion's two turbojets were attached to the bottom of the fuselage, and another remarkable feature was the mounting of massive fuel tanks at the tips of the wing. Later these tanks were replaced by pods containing fifty-two 2·75-in rockets as well as fuel. Later still each wingtip installation was arranged to accommodate 21 rockets and three Falcon missiles. As up to six more Falcons could be carried under the wing, the Scorpion was the most heavily armed fighter of its time. The final armament was two Genies, four Falcons and two rocket pods.

Famed principally for its airliners and bombers, the Douglas company built two remarkably contrasting fighters for the US Navy in the years following the war. The first of these, the F3D Skynight, was officially classed as a night fighter, as its name implies. This was a two-seater, the pilot and radar operator being seated side by side as in the Mosquito. A tunnel running from the cockpit through the bottom of the fuselage assisted them to bale out at high speed. The straight-wing twin-jet Skynight served with US Marine squadrons in Korea, where it destroyed more enemy aircraft than any other US Navy or Marine type.

The second of the Douglas fighters was the F4D Skyray, and this was very aptly named, for it resembled in form a deadly sting-ray. The wing was approximately of delta form, the rear, or trailing, edge being sweptback as well as the leading edge, and the tips being rounded. There were no horizontal tail surfaces. Late in 1953 a Skyray set up a world speed record of 752·9 mph, a notable advance on the previous one of 699·9 mph established by an F-86 Sabre during the previous year. The world speed record serves as a useful indication of the increase in fighter speed in post-war years. Thus, in 1946 a special Gloster Meteor became the first aircraft to exceed 600 mph, and in 1961 a McDonnell Phantom II became the first to fly at over 1,600 mph.

The names of ghosts and spirits now join the company of the cats, atmospheric disturbances, poisonous insects and the brotherhood of the Jolly Roger. The reason why construction of the McDonnell XFH-1 Phantom, already mentioned, was entrusted to a relatively unknown maker is that in 1943, when the order was placed, the big names were engaged in mass-producing fighters to meet the immediate demands of the war. Design studies for the new fighter were numerous, and there was one project with no fewer than eight tiny turbojets; the fighter which was actually built, and first flown in January 1945, had two Westinghouse axial-flow turbojets, housed in the much-thickened roots, or inner sections, of the straight wing.

The production-type FH-1 Phantom was succeeded in service by the F2H Banshee, similar in design but larger; but the F3H Demon was quite different in design, having one large Westinghouse turbojet which drew in air through cheek intakes in the fuselage sides. This turbojet proved very troublesome, and the Demon was not a great success. Next came the twin-jet sweptwing F-101 Voodoo for the USAF, in the design of which long range was emphasised, the type originally being classed as a penetration, or long-range escort, fighter. The F-101B development was a two-seater armed with three Falcon and two Genie missiles.

McDonnell's Voodoo must be considered as one of the outstanding fighters of its period (it first flew in 1954); but it was far less successful than the Phantom II, described later at some length as an eminent example of a truly modern fighter. Another fighter which will be selected for similar treatment is the Swedish SAAB Viggen, the ancestry of which must now be traced.

The coming of the Second World War left Sweden without a source for the supply of up-to-date fighters; so the Swedes decided to build one of their own. This came into being as the Flygförvaltningens (F.F.V.S.) J22, a well-designed monoplane which had a fine performance in spite of the low power of its Pratt & Whitney Twin Wasp piston engine. As the SAAB aircraft company was busy at that time building bomber and reconnaissance aircraft, the component parts of the J22 were farmed out to about 500 companies, mostly unconnected with aircraft construction. In July 1943, however, SAAB flew the J21, the first fighter of their own design. This was remarkable in being of twin-boom pusher type, with a German Daimler-Benz DB 605 piston engine; and as the design was broadly along the lines of the de Havilland Vampire it was comparatively easy to convert the aircraft for jet propulsion. Thus, with the de Havilland Goblin turbojet, as in the Vampire, the J21 became the J21R.

Sweden's SAAB J21R was powered with a British de Havilland ▶ Goblin turbojet. It was developed from the piston-engined J21.

For the next SAAB fighter, the J29, the de Havilland Ghost turbojet of greater thrust was chosen. The general shape of this sweptwing fighter is best described by recording that in Sweden it was known as Tunnan (the barrel). Next came the J32B all-weather fighter, a two-seater of quite normal design; but altogether extraordinary was the J35 Draken (Dragon) of 1955, this being of double-delta form. The meaning of this term, as applied to the Draken at least, is that the plan of the wing is composed of two triangles, the foremost one embodying the flattened air intakes for the Rolls-Royce Avon turbojet. Good field performance, by which is meant the ability to take-off and land in relatively short distances, is one of the Draken's strong points; ability to turn with unusual swiftness is another. Armament can include four Sidewinder missiles.

A French fighter comparable with Sweden's Draken is the Dassault Mirage III, but as this can have a rocket engine in addition to its turbojet it is described in the next chapter as an example of a modern mixed-power fighter. The ancestry of this very successful French fighter is a curious one and can be traced back to the Bloch MB-151 and MB-152, already mentioned as the equipment of French squadrons in 1940. This is explained by the fact that Marcel Bloch, the head of the constructing firm bearing his name, was deported by the Germans, and on his return to France in 1945 changed his name to Marcel Dassault.

The first fighter to bear the name Dassault was the straight-wing jet-propelled Ouragan (Hurricane) of 1949, and this was followed by the sweptwing Mystère and Super Mystère B-2. All three types were built in numbers and were exported, notably to Israel. In the service of the Israeli Air Force Mystère IVAs were in action during the Suez crisis of 1956. For the French Navy, Dassault developed the somewhat lighter and slower Étendard IV, the last deliveries of which were made in 1964.

Vautour (Vulture) was the fitting name of an aggressive-looking twin-jet two-seat all-weather fighter built by the SNCASO organisation. A special feature was the bicycle type of undercarriage, with two mainwheel units arranged in tandem, or one behind the other, under the fuselage. There were additionally small outrigger wheels under the wings.

With the coming of the Mystère series and the Vautour France had resumed a place of honour among the constructors of fighters, although competition for export orders was becoming keener. One reason for this was that a number of the less powerful countries were seeking to build fighters for themselves. Australia, where, during the war, the Boomerang single-seater had been built in numbers to designs originating with the North American com-

A particularly striking view of a SAAB Draken, showing four Hughes ▶
Falcon missiles and Swedish national markings. The circles and
three crowns are yellow and the remainder of the insignia blue.

pany, produced a version of the Sabre with Rolls-Royce Avon turbojet, entailing much redesign. Canada built, to her own designs, considerable numbers of a twin-jet all-weather fighter known as the Avro CF-100; even the Orenda turbojets were of Canadian design and manufacture. Among the distinctions achieved by the CF-100 was that of becoming the first straight-wing fighter in the world to exceed the speed of sound. This was achieved in a dive during 1952. The big Canadian two-seater was the first multi-seat all-weather fighter to serve with NATO (North Atlantic Treaty Organisation), the version concerned being the Mk 4B with all-rocket armament. This comprised a pod at each wingtip holding thirty 2·75-in rockets and a retractable pack in the bottom of the fuselage holding another forty-eight. CF-100s were supplied in some numbers to the Belgian Air Force. Before the war Belgium had herself produced some excellent biplane fighters, the single-seat Firefly and two-seat Fox, which originated with the British Fairey company, and after the war the Meteor and Hunter were put into production.

Italy has maintained a place among the world's successful designers of fighter aircraft with the G.91 series of single-jet and twin-jet monoplanes; but these are in reality tactical fighters or strike fighters, or what are perhaps best described as ground-attack and reconnaissance aircraft, and call for no detailed comment here.

In India a twin-jet fighter known as the Hindustan HF-24 Marut (Wind Spirit) and designed by a team headed by the Fw 190 designer Kurt Tank has been put into production. This German-designed, Indian-built, fighter was planned to have Egyptian turbojets based on the British Bristol Siddeley Orpheus and be armed with Russian guided missiles or French unguided rockets in addition to British cannon. The Egyptian turbojet mentioned was originally developed for a fighter which originated in Spain according to the ideas of the German Professor Willy Messerschmitt and was taken over by the United Arab Republic for development near Cairo. Interesting though such projects are it must be recognised that responsibility for the design and development of truly modern fighters must rest increasingly in the hands of the World Powers, so elaborate and expensive are these aircraft. This will become clear in the final chapters.

	Span	Length	Seats	Loaded weight	Maximum speed	Service ceiling	Armament
USA							
Grumman F7F-1 Tigercat	51′ 6″	45′ 4″	1	22,560 lb	427 mph	36,200 ft	4 c+4 h m-g
Grumman F11F-1 Tiger	31′ 7″	44′ 11″	1	24,078 lb	890 mph	50,500 ft	4 c+2 or 4 g m
Lockheed P-80A Shooting Star	39′ 11″	34′ 6″	1	14,500 lb	558 mph	45,000 ft	6 h m-g
Lockheed F-104G Starfighter	21′ 11″	54′ 9″	1	28,779 lb	1,450 mph	58,000 ft	1 rev'r c+6 g m
North American F-86A Sabre	37′ 1″	37′ 6″	1	16,357 lb	675 mph	48,300 ft	6 h m-g
North American F-100D Super Sabre	38′ 9″	47′ 0″	1	34,830 lb	864 mph	44,900 ft	4 c
Republic P-84E Thunderjet	36′ 5″	38′ 6″	1	22,460 lb	613 mph	43,200 ft	6 h m-g
Republic F-105D Thunderchief	34′ 11″	67′ 0″	1	52,546 lb	1,390 mph	50,000 ft	1 rev'r c+4 g m
Vought F7U-3 Cutlass	38′ 8″	44′ 3″	1	31,640 lb	610 mph	40,000 ft	4 c+4 g m
Convair F-106A Delta Dart	38′ 3″	70′ 9″	1	38,250 lb	1,525 mph	57,000 ft	4–6 g m
Douglas F4D Skyray	33′ 6″	45′ 8″	1	27,000 lb	695 mph	48,000 ft	4 c+4 g m
McDonnell F-101B Voodoo	39′ 8″	67′ 5″	2	46,500 lb	1,220 mph	51,000 ft	5 g m
SWEDEN							
SAAB J35F Draken	30′ 10″	50′ 4″	1	25,130 lb	Mach 2	70,000 ft	2 c+4 g m
FRANCE							
Dassault Super Mystère B-2	34′ 6″	46′ 1″	1	22,050 lb	743 mph	55,750 ft	2 c+2 g m
SO Vautour IIN	49′ 7″	52′ 0″	2	45,635 lb	685 mph	50,000 ft	4 c+4 g m
CANADA							
Avro CF-100 Mk 4B	53′ 7″	54′ 2″	2	35,500 lb	650 mph	40,000+ft	108 u-g m

11

Men and Machines Today

With the story of fighter development now carried to the point where ordinary squadron aircraft exceed 1,500 mph, and before examining some of today's more notable types in greater detail, some further consideration may be given to the men who fly them. The last items of safety equipment recorded were the parachute, which came into general use in the 1920s, and the ejection seat, as generally introduced after the Second World War. In connection with this type of seat reference has been made to the effect on pilots of g, or gravity, in high-speed manoeuvres. As speeds increased above 300 mph or so pilots began more frequently to black out, or become temporarily unconscious, during rapid changes of direction, the reason for this being the draining of blood from the brain. To counteract this effect the g-suit was introduced, and is now a normal item of apparel. The g-suit contains bladders which fit over the lower parts of the wearer's body, and which, when the g forces or loads have built up to a certain degree, are inflated by compressed air, thus preventing the blood from draining away. As a precaution against failure of the cabin pressurising system the automatically inflating pressure suit has been introduced, and clad in this, together with his glass-fibre helmet, or bone dome, and special boots to protect him in case of ejection, today's fighter pilot presents a figure quite in harmony with the fantastic aeroplanes he flies.

Among these aeroplanes the British Aircraft Corporation Lightning, the RAF's standard all-weather intercepter, ranks high, although the basic design is over twenty years old. Several variants, or different models, have been built, but common to all are the very sharply sweptback wing and horizontal tail

Peeling off from an echelon formation, these BAC Lightning F Mk 6 ▶
twin-jet single-seat fighters display their massive finned ventral pack
for fuel and guns and Firestreak missiles on the fuselage sides.

surfaces. While the wing, which has five spars, or transverse internal structural members, is attached near the centreline of the fuselage, as seen in side view, the horizontal tail surfaces are attached almost at the bottom. Following the general pattern adopted for high-speed aircraft these surfaces do not comprise the time-honoured fixed tailplane and movable elevator, which serve respectively to provide stability and cause the aircraft to climb and dive. Instead the surfaces are in a single piece, all of which moves. This is known as the all-moving, all-flying or slab type of surface, and is sometimes called an elevator and sometimes a tailplane. Another feature which the Lightning shares with other modern fighters is the powered system for operating the control surfaces, necessitated by the tremendous air pressure at high speed. Integral fuel tanks, or tanks formed by the wing structure itself, are located not only in the wing but in the flaps also. Three additional jettisonable tanks can be fitted, one very large one under the fuselage and two carried not under the wing, as is usual on fighters, but above it. In this position the tanks do not interfere with the retraction of the under-carriage into the wing in an outward direction – another uncommon feature.

The fuselage of the Lightning is very deep, and this is because the two Rolls-Royce Avon turbojets are superimposed, or mounted one above the other,

being also staggered, or positioned one ahead of the other. Far removed from the engines is the air intake in the extreme nose, and projecting even ahead of this is the conical centre-body which houses the radar. Although it is not a carrier-borne fighter the Lightning, in its Mark 6 form, shares with some other modern fighters the distinction of having an arrester hook. This is for emergency use at suitably equipped airfields and is used to stop the aircraft from running off the end of the runway on landing. Several different armament combinations are possible on the Lightning fighter, including guided missiles of the Hawker Siddeley Firestreak or Red Top type. The Red Top is the later model; it flies at Mach 3 and has a range of seven miles. For ground-attack work the Lightning has been developed with other special armament schemes; but it is here considered as a pre-eminent example of the intercepter fighter, a class which the RAF introduced with the Hawker Fury of the early 1930s.

Interception is one of many tasks assigned to the McDonnell Phantom II, sometimes called McDonnell Douglas Phantom II, for the two great companies were merged in 1967. This aeroplane is known to the US Navy, Marine Corps and USAF as the F-4, and its extreme versatility in the fighting, ground-attack and reconnaissance rôles is further extended by its ability to operate from aircraft

This McDonnell Douglas F4-B Phantom II is glimpsed at the very instant of departure from an aircraft carrier.
The Phantom II is beyond question one of the most successful fighters of all time.

carriers. From the outset of flight trials, which began on 27 May 1958, the type showed the highest promise, and a Mach number of 2·6 was a remarkable early attainment for a fighter which, in appearance, can hardly be described as sleek. One envious aircraft designer was heard to declare on first seeing a Phantom II that it must have achieved its performance by 'brute force and ignorance'. Everything about this fighter, indeed, gives an impression of massive power and strength; but the record of the McDonnell Division of McDonnell Douglas in building fighters was never one of ignorance, though troubles were experienced with the Demon.

The normal powerplant of the Phantom II consists of two General Electric J79 turbojets, the air for which is taken in through two very deep elephant ear ducts projecting from the fuselage sides in line with the rear cockpit, for the aircraft is a two-seater. To meet the requirements of Britain's Royal Navy two Rolls-Royce Spey turbofans have been installed. This type of engine is half-way between a turbojet and a propeller-turbine, the internal fan accelerating rearwards a smaller mass of air than the airscrew of a propeller-turbine but more than the compressor of a turbojet. Fuel economy is a virtue of such engines, and this is one reason for the Royal Navy's choice, having regard to the long over-water flights undertaken. In order to take in the extra air for the fans the intakes on the Royal Navy Phantom IIs have been made six inches wider.

There are other very distinctive features of the Phantom II. The long pointed nose, for example, has a marked drooping appearance, due in part for the need to give the pilot the best possible view for deck landing and also to the seating of the second crewman on a higher level. The effect is heightened further when a 20-mm 'revolver cannon' is carried, for this is housed in a kind of chin under the nose. Even more striking is the marked dihedral angle (upward inclination) of the outer sections of the wing, which fold upwards for stowage aboard an aircraft carrier, contrasting very sharply with the even more pronounced anhedral angle (downward inclination) of the all-moving horizontal tail surfaces. The immense strength which must be built in to such a fast and massive fighter is suggested by the fact that the wing

skin is machined from panels $2\frac{1}{2}$ inches thick. Armament can include six Sparrow guided missiles or four Sparrows and four Sidewinders, carried in the bottom of the fuselage, semi-internally, and under the wings. The electronic equipment includes a navigation computer, a package installation which deals with communications and navigation and also enables the aircraft to identify itself to friendly forces, and an automatic radar fire-control, or weapon-launching, system.

The Phantom II is ghostly only in name and in the speed with which it can disappear from sight, and a similar observation might be made concerning France's Dassault Mirage III. This small delta-wing fighter could not justly be described as a *type jockey*, although it had its origins in a French Air Force requirement for a lighter type of fighter than was becoming common. It has met with very great success as a fighter, fighter-bomber and reconnaissance aircraft but is considered here as a mixed-power intercepter.

In addition to its SNECMA Atar turbojet the Mirage III can be fitted with a rocket engine designed by the Société d'Étude de la Propulsion par Réaction, and known as the SEPR 844. This is produced as a self-contained pack which fits on the bottom of the fuselage and can be jettisoned when the liquid fuel, or propellant, is exhausted after 80

The searing flame from the rocket engine accentuates the deadly appearance of this missile-armed Dassault Mirage III. This picture may be compared with that of a Mirage IV in the companion volume *The World's Bombers*.

seconds. The dry weight, without fuel, is 200 lb and the total weight 500 lb. The Mirage III intercepter has provision for one MATRA R.530 guided missile under the fuselage, two Sidewinders under the wing, and, if required, two 30-mm cannon in the fuselage. Swiss Air Force Mirage IIIs carry Falcon missiles.

There is no indication that rocket engines are likely to be used by fighters of the future, and certainly no provision has been made for one in the

SAAB-37 Viggen (Thunderbolt), due to replace the Draken in Swedish squadrons in the mid-1970s. Like the Draken, the Viggen is of double-delta form, but differs greatly in arrangement. There are, in fact, two separate surfaces essentially triangular in shape. The first of these is known as the foreplane or nose-plane, and carries flaps; the main wing carries elevons, or surfaces which act both as ailerons for lateral control and elevators. This remarkable design accounts largely for the Viggen's astonishing field performance, for although its top speed is above Mach 2 it can operate from runways little more than 500 yards long. In Sweden these runways often consist of nothing more than a straight stretch of road.

Mention remains to be made of the Northrop F-5, which, although weighing less than half as much as a Phantom II, has two turbojets. Offering excellent value for money it has been widely exported; but its

armament of two Sidewinders and two cannon, and its Mach number of 1·4, proclaim that it is, as already noted, a compromise. Certainly the F-5 contrasts sharply with a Russian Tupolev fighter which is by far the largest and heaviest in service. Bearing the NATO code-name Fiddler this massive twin-jet all-weather intercepter is estimated to weigh 100,000 lb. No *type jockey* could do the job of this monster, with its advanced radar and four large missiles allied with a Mach number of about 1·75.

	Span	Length	Seats	Loaded weight	Maximum speed	Service ceiling	Armament
GREAT BRITAIN							
BAC Lightning	34′ 10″	55′ 3″	1	*	Mach 2+	*	2 g m
USA							
McDonnell Phantom II	38′ 5″	58′ 3″	2	46,000 lb	Mach 2+	70,000 ft	6–8 g m
Northrop F-5	25′ 3″	47′ 2″	1	20,576 lb	Mach 1·4	50,000+ft	2 c+2 g m
FRANCE							
Dassault Mirage III	27′ 7″	49′ 3″	1	27,115 lb	Mach 2·2	65,600 ft	2 c+3 g m
SWEDEN							
SAAB Viggen	34′ 9″	53′ 6″	1	35,275 lb	Mach 2+	*	Several g m

* Data not available.

12

What Might Have Been, What May Be

In general the fighters named in the preceding pages were brought to the operational stage: that is, they entered service with squadrons. A number of types which did see squadron service receive no mention for reasons of space, and these include the Austrian Hansa-Brandenburg and Phönix and the French Hanriot and German Roland types of the First World War and the Czechoslovak Aeros and Avias of later years. Only in one or two instances has mention been made of prototypes, or experimental pattern aircraft, which, for one reason or another, were never made in any quantity. There were hundreds of such prototypes, and from these a few are selected for special mention by reason of their exceptional interest.

Between the wars Britain was not alone in experimenting with large fighters armed with two 37-mm cannon. Bell, a company which could always be looked to for something out of the ordinary, built during the 1930s the Airacuda, which had two such guns, one in the front of each engine nacelle; and for each of these there was a gunner. Nor were the Me 163 and Vought Cutlass the first fighters to have no horizontal tail surfaces, for in Britain Westland had previously built the Pterodactyl V, which, having no tail whatever, offered the gunner an unequalled field of fire. The Italian Macchis mentioned were not the last fighter flying-boats, for in 1947 the Saunders-Roe company built and flew in Britain the world's first jet-propelled flying-boat, a twin-jet fighter. Even more remarkable was the Convair Sea Dart, a fighter which floated on its fuselage and took-off and alighted on retractable ski-like surfaces called hydro-skis. And lest it be supposed that the parasite fighters previously mentioned (those carried by other aircraft) were the last of their kind, then allusion must be made to the jet-propelled McDonnell XF-85, launched from a Boeing Superfortress in 1948.

Some curious engines and arrangements of engines were also to be seen on fighters: thus, a Lockheed Shooting Star was tested with two ramjet engines, one on each wingtip. (The ramjet is the simplest form of engine, consisting of a tube into which air is rammed at the front by the forward speed of the aircraft and burnt continuously with fuel; but it can only function at high speed.) There was, too, a fighter with one engine at the front driving a tractor airscrew and another at the rear acting as a pusher. This was the Dornier Do 335. But perhaps the most astonishing fighters of all were the tailsitters, which sat on their tails for take-off and landing, the most successful of which was the Convair XFY-1. This fighter had a propeller-turbine driving two co-axial contra-rotating airscrews. This type of engine is similar to a turbojet except that the gases produced in the combustion chamber not only drive the compressor but an airscrew as well. By co-axial is meant on the same axis; contra-rotating means rotating in opposite directions. The most amazing of all the tailsitters was the Bachem Natter (Viper), on test in Germany as the war ended. This rocket-propelled fighter was launched vertically from rails. Having climbed

towards a bomber formation at over 35,000 ft a minute it would discharge a mass of rocket projectiles from its nose. The pilot would then use his ejection seat and at the same time the section of the fuselage housing the rocket engine would break off and descend by parachute.

Could fantasy go further? Not, it appears, in the years immediately ahead, for the fighters now in prospect are relatively conventional in design. Indeed, the intended Dassault successor to the Mirage III is no longer of delta type but has normal wing and tail surfaces. It is true that several types of aircraft now being developed, and sometimes referred to as fighters, are very unusual indeed, some being of the so-called swing-wing type, the sweepback angle of the wing being variable in flight, and others having VTOL (vertical take-off and landing) capability. But these are either purely experimental or are mainly intended for ground-attack, or strike duties.

The super-fighters of the future will probably be American and Russian. Although a specialised fighter version of the swing-wing General Dynamics F-111, intended for the US Navy, has been abandoned, and further development of the USAF's Lockheed YF-12A experimental Mach 3 intercepter seems unlikely, both the Services concerned have announced their future plans. For the Navy Grumman will build the F-14, a two-seat swing-wing type with two turbofans, and likely to be armed with Hughes Phoenix missiles. The Phoenix is a long-range weapon weighing about 1,000 lb. The choice of the USAF is the McDonnell Douglas F-15, and although in recent years the future of the fighter has often been in doubt because of improvements in ground-to-air missiles, the USAF leaves no doubt of its own views. The USAF Vice-Chief of Staff has said: 'The new family of Soviet fighters are the forerunners of our possible air opposition in the mid- and late 1970s. By 1975 the basic technology of the F-4E Phantom, our best air-to-air fighter, will be twenty years old. The new Soviet fighters promise to outclass the F-4 in terms of manoeuvrability, acceleration and weaponry.'

The new Soviet fighters mentioned may well be versions of the MiG-23, claimed to be capable of Mach 3 and dating from 1965 or earlier. A fixed-wing type, this has twin tail fins and huge sloping air intakes for its two turbojets.

The F-15 will bear a startling resemblance to it.

FURTHER READING

British Aeroplanes 1914–1918, J. M. Bruce, Putnam, 1969.

British Fighter since 1912, The, Peter Lewis, Putnam, 1965.

Combat Aircraft of the World, edited and compiled by John W. R. Taylor, Ebury Press and Michael Joseph, 1969.

Jane's All the World's Aircraft, edited by John W. R. Taylor, Sampson Low Marston & Co Ltd. Annual.

Warplanes of the First World War: Fighters. (Three volumes), J. M. Bruce, Macdonald, 1965, 1968, 1969.

Warplanes of the Second World War: Fighters. (Four volumes), William Green, Macdonald, 1961.

INDEX